THE COMPOSITE CHART

The Horoscope of a Relationship

BY JOHN·TOWNLEY

Edited by Christine Townley

SAMUEL WEISER, INC.
New York, N. Y.
1974

Printed in U.S.A. by
NOBLE OFFSET PRINTERS, INC.
New York, N.Y. 10003

DEDICATION

to my parents, without whose faithful support I would long ago have starved . . .

and,

to Al H. Morrison, my mentor, colleague, and friend, who started me on this road,

with special thanks to Ms. Christine Janis who prodded me into writing this by threatening to co-author it.

The Composite Chart— Introduction

Of all the astrological techniques I have worked with, I have gotten more use and enjoyment out of composite charts than any other. Essentially, a composite chart is just a horoscope of the mutual midpoints of two natal charts. It seems to describe the entity that is, between two people (or more), *the relationship itself*. It charts, by transit and progression, the success and happiness or the difficulties and sorrows of any given relationship, be it marriage, friendship, business partnership, or politics.

For such an invaluable technique, composites are virtually unknown in the U.S.A. I first was told about it on the First Avenue bus by former Astrologers' Guild Trustee Arlene Plakun (many thanks, Arlene!). She had learned about it at a previous ISAR symposium, but did not know the origin of the idea. Since then I have traced it through German astrologer Edith Wangemann as far back as the great Dr. Walter Koch, originator of the GOH Birthplace House System, who may also have been the originator of the composite chart.

Here following, I have set down in as brief a form as possible the how's and why's of composite technique and some of its future possibilities, including numerous examples. It will serve as a start, but the only way you can really investigate the validity of this tool is to *try it yourself*. It is all very interesting and hypothetical to read about, but I guarantee if you actually take the energy to use it yourself for a while, it will blow your mind. Happy landings . . .

—John Townley

Technical Note

The angles and house cusps of the horoscopes in this work are all rounded off to the nearest ¼ degree, unless the chart has been rectified. It is something of an astrological conceit, I believe, to appear to be terribly accurate in this area when a chart is unrectified, even when hospital birth time is available. Rectification is the *only* process by which one may derive true functioning angles to within a minute of arc. This is not, of course, the case with horary and electional charts, where initial precision is of the utmost importance.

All charts use the Koch GOH, or Birthplace, House system. The system is based upon the division of time along the prime vertical, and seems to be especially effective in the timing of events. Most house systems seem to work fairly well in one fashion or another, largely depending upon how the astrologer looks at them and what is demanded of them. Feel free to convert these charts to your own favorite system and see if they work better for you.

Calculating the Composite Chart

Calculating the Composite Chart

Since the composite chart is a chart made up of midpoints, one must first be familiar with the calculation of midpoints. Between any two points on a circle (in our case, the Zodiac) there are two other points between them which are equidistant from them. In Figure One, points C and D are both equidistant from points A and B. Thus, C and D are said to be the midpoints of A and B. Since the distance ACB is shorter than ADB, C is called the *near* midpoint, and D is called the *far* midpoint. Composite charts use exclusively the near midpoint.

Calculating midpoints—In order to calculate midpoints with maximum ease, first it is necessary to convert the degree of any given sign into its equivalent on a 360° dial (see Figure Two). Thus, for instance, 15° Taurus becomes just plain 45° and 23° Sagittarius becomes 264°. To determine the midpoint between these two degrees, add them and divide the sum by two:

$$15° \text{ Taurus}— \qquad 45$$
$$23° \text{ Sagittarius}— \quad \underline{263}$$
$$308$$

308 divided by 2 equals 159,
which reconverts to 9° Virgo

Virgo, however, is the far midpoint, so we take its opposite, 9° Pisces, for the near midpoint (near and far midpoints are always opposite each other).

The Composite Chart—In order to determine the houses of the composite chart, we must first find the near midpoint between the midheavens of the two natal charts concerned. In this case, the midpoint between Franklin D. Roosevelt's midheaven (23° Gemini, Fig 3) and Eleanor Roosevelt's Midheaven (19° Virgo, Fig. 4) is 6° Leo. In review, this was determined so:

$$\text{plus} \quad 23° \text{ Gemini, or} \quad 83$$
$$19° \text{ Virgo, or} \quad \underline{169}$$
$$252$$

252 divided by 2 equals 126,
or 6° Leo

6° Leo is the midheaven of the composite chart. To determine
the rest of the composite house cusps, read them off from your
table of houses as you normally would using the *latitude at
which the relationship primarily functions*. In this case, the
latitude of Washington, D.C. is used, yielding an ascendant in the
first degree of Scorpio (Fig.5). Had we been concerned with the
couple's relationship before they moved to Washington, the
latitude of their New York home at Hyde Park would have been
used, yielding the last degree of Libra on the ascendant and
describing a different sort of relationship.

This method of using only the MC/MC midpoint instead of the
midpoints of all the house cusps is the easiest and most valuable
way of approaching composite houses, as it makes the chart
latitude-sensitive and avoids the impossible house cusps that
would often arise otherwise.*see footnote

To determine the composite Lights and planets, find the
midpoints between identical bodies in the natal charts. Thus, the
Sun/Sun midpoint becomes the composite Sun, the Moon/Moon
midpoint becomes the composite Moon, and so on through the
rest of the planets and nodes.

In the composite of FDR and Eleanor, a nice description of
their relationship may be found. Venus rising gives a very
charming view to the outsider and Leo on the MC lends an
outgoing and sunny reputation. Sun closely conjuct Mercury

-----

* In constructing the houses of the composite chart I have used
only the midpoint of the two natal midheavens and not also the
midpoint of the two natal ascendants to avoid geometrically
impossible situations such as: at 41°N, a natal MC of 15°
Capricorn would yield an asc. of 28° Aries. An MC of 20° yields
an asc. of 17° Libra. The near midpoint of 15° Capricorn and
20° Cancer (the two MC's) is 17½° Libra, but but the near
midpoint of 28° Aries and 17° Libra is 22½° Cancer. One cannot
have a Libra MC with Cancer rising! This is the result of the
earth's tilt and the resulting variance in ascending speeds of the
different signs.

This midpoint between ascendants is a very relevant point,
however, as I have only recently found out. I suggest inserting it
into the composite chart as you would the Vertex (one might try
a true composite vertex, as well). It will usually fall in the 1st or
12th house, though occassionally (as in the example above) in
the 6th or 7th. It is the real composite ascendant that does not
vary, while the one you read from the house tables is more
locational and changes with latitude.

makes for a very close meeting of minds and a sharp flow of intellect, but primarily at a intuitive and gut level as the chart lacks air. Moon-Jupiter conjunct in Cancer in the ninth describe a tremendous concern for education, welfare (sic), and the general good and care of the people—the touchstones of modern Liberalism. Mars and Uranus in Virgo in the eleventh describe the intellectual and oddball (for the time) company the couple socialized with. Neptune opposing Venus from the seventh, however, describes the idealization of the marriage by the public and ease with which marital difficulties were concealed (Neptune rules the fifth—infidelity). Pluto and Saturn conjunct at the cusp of the eighth describe the deeper pain and fears in the relationship, particularly concerning sexuality (the eighth). And so on . . .

If composite charts are to be of use, they should respond to transits, thus allowing us to confirm by the composite other transits applying to the natal charts. In the months preceding his death, FDR's natal chart had been undergoing heavy afflictions by transit which describe his increasing poor health at that time. People daily manage to survive the most dire transiting afflictions, however, so there is no really reliable way to forecast the death of an individual. In a marriage, though, the relationship must of necessity die with the death of one of the partners, so we must look to the composite to find if it is as afflicted by transit as the natal chart.

On the day of FDR's death, April 12, 1945: Sun and Moon were at 22° Aries with Mercury at 23° Aries, quincunx composite Uranus. He died of a stroke—sudden death (Uranus) involving the brain (Mercury). Mars (14° Pisces) opposed Jupiter (19° Virgo) mutually squaring composite Sun and Mercury. Saturn was at 5° Cancer, approaching composite Jupiter, Uranus (10° Gemini) on composite vertex, and Pluto (8° Leo) on composite MC. For these reasons it could be surmised that the relationship might be about to terminate, and by referring to the natal charts it could be determined that this would more likely be for reasons of health rather than incompatability.

Composite charts respond quite predictibly to transits, and their progress often seems quite spectacular, as most events in the relationship will be triggered by transiting *conjunctions* or *oppositions*, rather than by lesser aspects. This is probably because bodies in a composite chart are really just midpoints, and midpoints respond better to the conjuction or opposition (a conjunction to a near midpoint is an opposition to a far one, so really we are dealing exclusively with the conjuction).

Interpretation and transits of composite charts is basically the same as standard natal technique, but it must always be kept in mind that it is a chart of a *relationship* and not of a physical person. It will not tell you what is going on in either person's life, but only how these factors effect the relationship between the two. This is sometimes a very subtle difference, and only experience and looking at a lot of composites over a period of time will lead to accurate delineation, as is the case with any astrological technique.

Comparisons between each of the natal charts and the resulting composite can be quite fruitful, as well. For instance, if the composite Saturn were on one partner's Sun, the relationship might tend to stabilize that person, or, if afflicted, highly restrict him. Or again, if the composite Sun fell on one partner's Mars, that person might provide the main energy and initiation in the relationship.

Probably the most important single factor in composite interpretation is house position. The house position of the Lights or an important stellium in a composite will often be the determining factor in its character. A brief round of examples:

First House—The Lights or an important stellium here makes for a very noticable relationship as seen by others. "A perfect match," "How well they look together," etc. Particularly with Sun conjunct Ascendant.

Second House—A monetary or business relationship. Not necessarily people who make a lot of money, but whose primary orientation shows concern with the importance of material things.

Third House—An intellectual relationship—much communication on the mental level, creativity in ideas.

Fourth House—Homebodies. Keeping house and raising children.

Fifth House—Usually a heavy emphasis on sex. Not often good for long-range partnership, but great for an affair.

Sixth House—This is a difficult place, sharing much with the twelfth. Usually this is two people thrown together to learn from their mistakes. I have not yet seen a sixth house Sun composite where the relationship has not eventually broken up, though some may last for quite a while before this happens. It might mean serving together in some physical capacity, but I have not got a composite for a butler and a maid (for instance) to test that possibility.

Seventh House—This seems the best house for a good marriage these days. It forces both partners into a truly one-to-one equal relationship. Not an ideal in Victorian times, but to be desired today. Where one fails, the other makes up. Both sides of an issue come out and, hopefully, synthesize.

Eighth House——Like the second, concern with physical goods, but in a more receptive sense/ e.g., the eighth house inherits money, while the second makes its own.

Ninth House—Much concern for ideals, philosophy, etc. Good mental communication. Also travel—often found in couples in the diplomacy who must travel a lot.

Tenth House—Career, business partnership. Good for partners in a company, or for couples where both partners are professionals.

Eleventh House—A very friendly relationship, with concern for the beauty and trappings of being related. Sexual (if a couple) but not as physical or intense as the fifth house.

Twelfth House—All that applies to the sixth, but heavier. Sixth house relationships are frequently a learning ground from whence both parties move on the wiser, but the twelfth is more self-destructive and harder to become disattached from. To be avoided from the start, if possible.

Interpretation of the house positions will vary, of course, according to aspect. A seventh house Sun that is heavily afflicted will bring a fight for equality rather than a real one-to-one relationship, for instance. In the end, everything must be taken into account before a judgement is made, as in natal astrology.

Figure 1

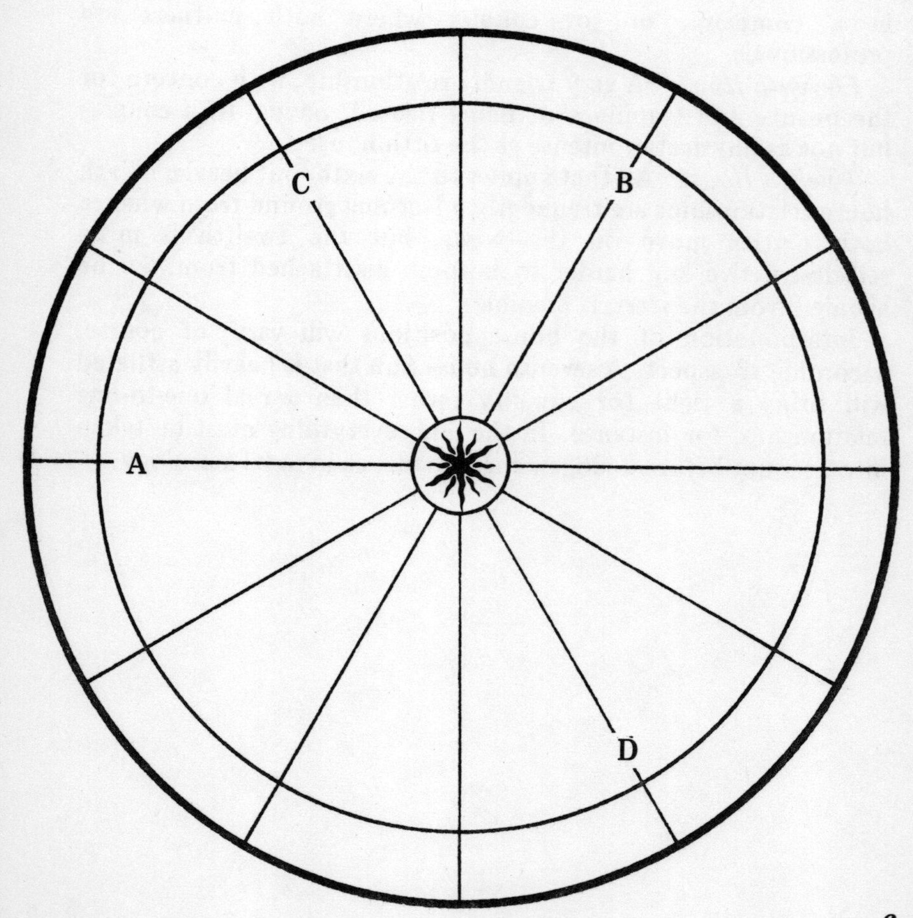

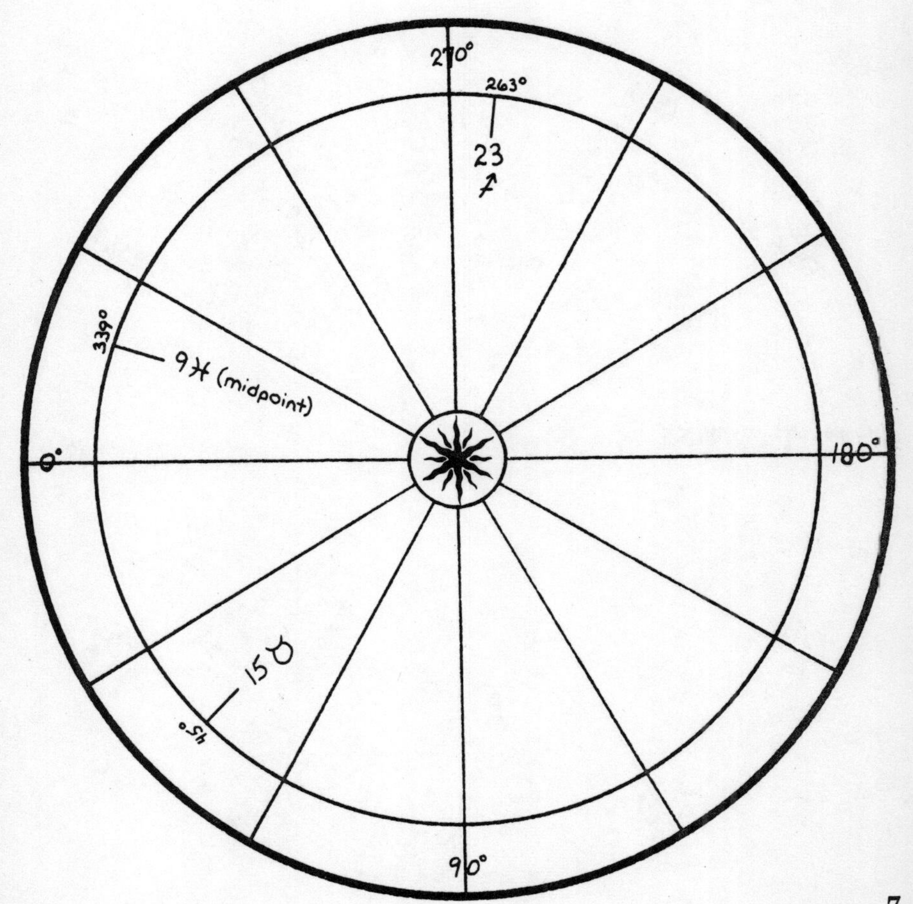

270°
263°
23
♐
339°
9♃ (midpoint)
0°
180°
15♉
45°
90°

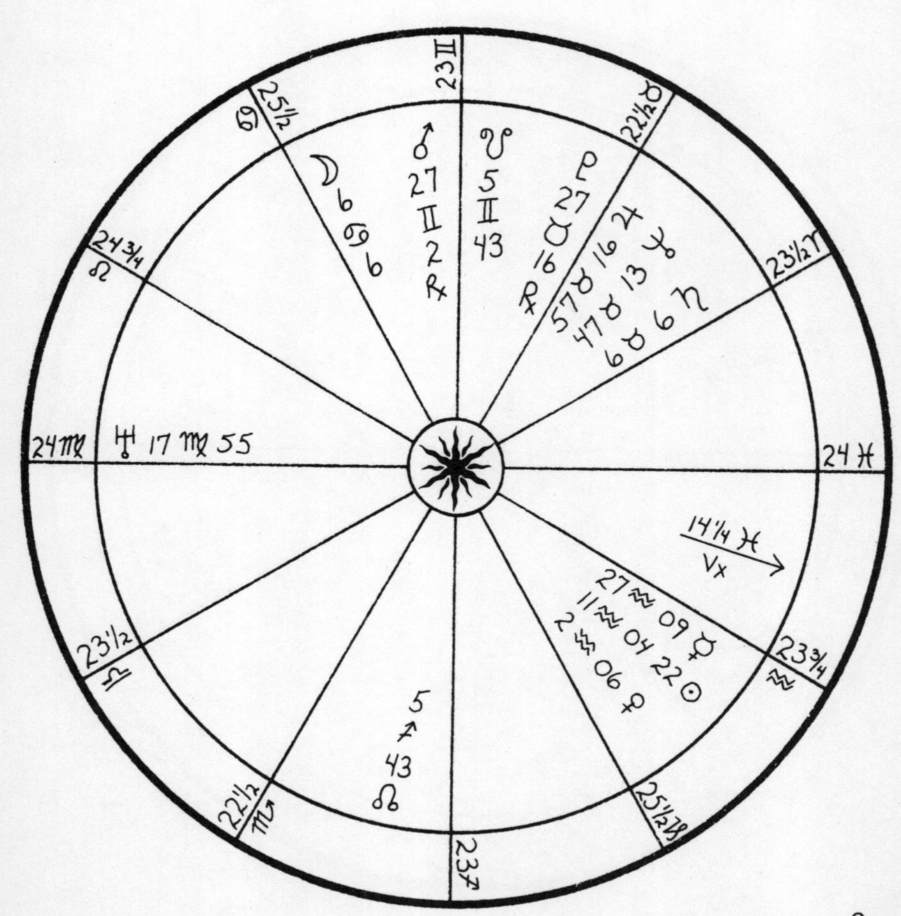

Figure 3
F.D. Roosevelt
30 January 1882
8:45 P.M.
Hyde Park, N.Y.
Koch GOH Houses

Figure 4
Eleanor Roosevelt
11 October 1884
New York City
From M.E. Jones
Koch GOH Houses

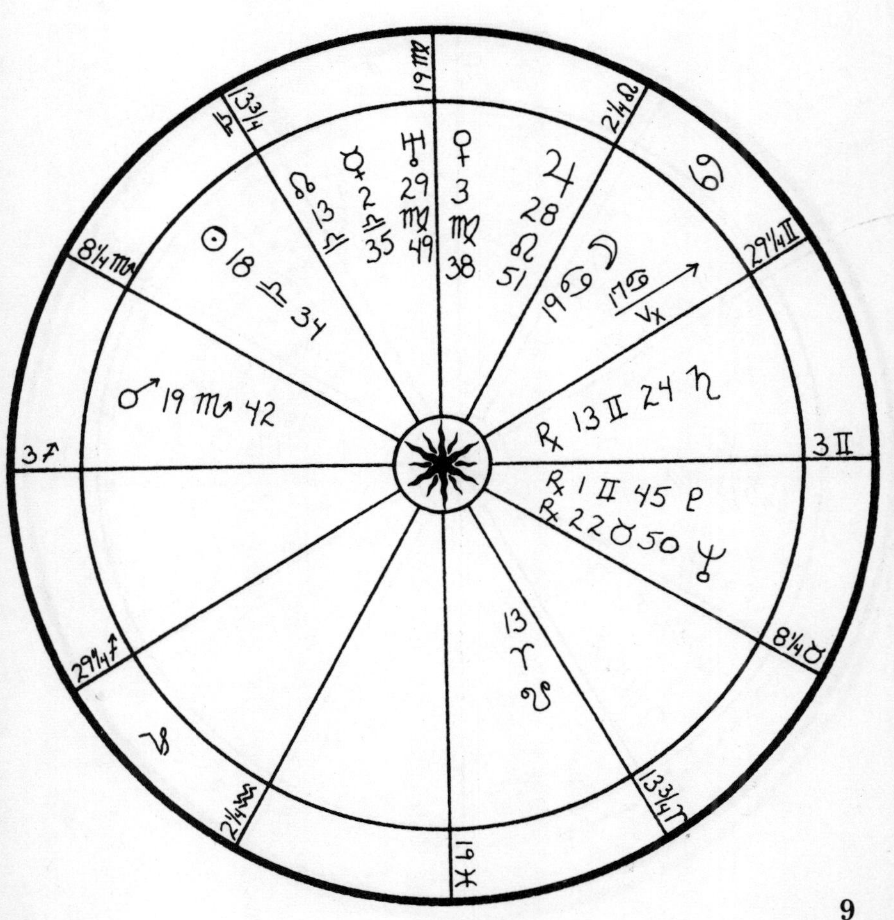

9

Figure 5
Composite
F.D.R. and Eleanor
Washington, D.C.
Koch GOH Houses

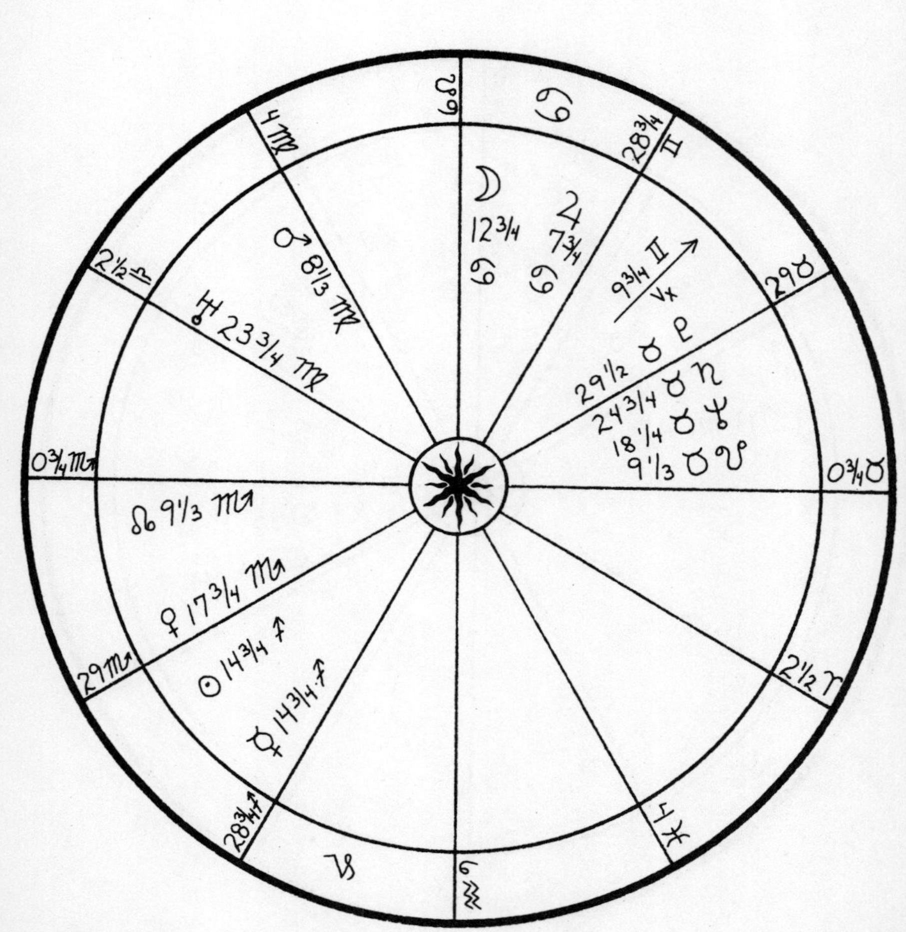

The Progressed Composite
and the Composite Solar Return

The Progressed Composite and the Composite Solar Return

To construct the progressed composite: first progress the individual natal charts to whatever date you are concerned with, progressing the midheaven by true solar arc. Then take the near midpoint between the two progressed midheavens and use that as the midheaven for a new progressed composite, filling in the rest of the house cusps as you normally would using the latitude at which the natives are living. Take the midpoint of the two progressed Suns, Moons, etc. and place them in the chart just as you would in a natal composite.

For example, we have the natal composite of a couple (fig. 6) and their progressed composite for the month in which they split up (fig. 7) and as a result became divorced. To begin with, the natal composite is not very auspicious. Moon in the 12th is never good, and here Mars exactly squares a stellium of Neptune, Mercury, and Jupiter, angular. The relationship was filled with contentiousness and endless disputes over usually pointless matters. A strong seventh house is usually good, tending to put the partners into equality, but here, because of the square, it manifested as a battle for supremacy. At the time of the breakup, transiting Saturn goes over the composite ascendant and transiting Jupiter opposes the MC. Something is obviously afoot.

Moving to the progressed composite—the vertex is applying to a conjunction with the Sun, so something fateful and largely beyond the control of either partner (emotionally speaking, as we are dealing with progressions) is about to happen. The Moon is void-of-course on its way to changing signs, indicating a new emotional tenor about to enter the relationship. As transiting Saturn is opposing the progressed composite Venus in the 5th, we may imply that this change is going to be for the worse, taking into account as well the difficult transits to the natal composite. (It is interesting to note here that the degree of the prog. comp. vertex is exactly that of the composite Sun of the man and his *next* wife and the natal Sun of their son born four years later! It's all in the cards, folks . . .)

Another way to triple check all this is to do the most recent solar return chart for the natal composite. This is done the same way any normal solar return is constructed, merely requiring one to have calculated the composite Sun exact to the second of arc. In this case (fig. 8), we see Venus on the ascendant, which at first looks nice (the couple were very active in the entertainment business that year and often favorably before the public). The rest, however, is not so good. Mars-Neptune in Scorpio is deceit, unfaithfulness. Saturn on the 5th cusp opposing Uranus, Pluto, and Mercury further augment this. Jupiter square the Sun would suggest an unsettling year, and the general lack of air (only a very late Jupiter) and fire suggest goings on that do not get a proper verbal airing. A loose grand water trine with the focus on the Saturn-outer planet opposition suggest that nothing is done about the difficulties, but rather they are taken for granted (as in natal astrology—a grand trine tied in with a major affliction makes for people to don't bother to rise to the occasion.)

All in all, we have now three major indicators that this would be a difficult year for the couple, focusing on the month of March, 1966. At this point astrology ends, and marriage counselling begins.

In this case, all counselling, psychiatric and otherwise, was in vain, and divorce was inevitable. As it turned out, it was quite an amicable settlement with minimum payments involved and custody of the daughter going to the mother. This is not always the case with divorces, so it might be of use to see if composite techniques could give us a clue as to which parent would get the child.

First the composite of mother and daughter (fig. 9): Sun, Venus, Mercury in the 2nd suggest a monetary relationship, and four planets in the 9th suggest education. Moon in the 6th in trine with the Sun and the MC suggest physical care and feeding. So far, it looks like the mother is favored. Looking at the father-daughter composite: (fig. 10) three planets in the 12th, Saturn on the MC with Venus, Pluto rising, and Moon opposing the ascendant. This does not look like the close, physical, working relationship that custody would imply. The father might, at a later date, have real influence on the daughter's career, but we can fairly definitely say that custody would go to the mother, as was the case.

This is a somewhat unusual application of parent-child composite work, but such composites are always of great interest and use in clarifying the relationships between parents and their children.

Figure 6
Composite
Couple
New York City
Koch GOH Houses

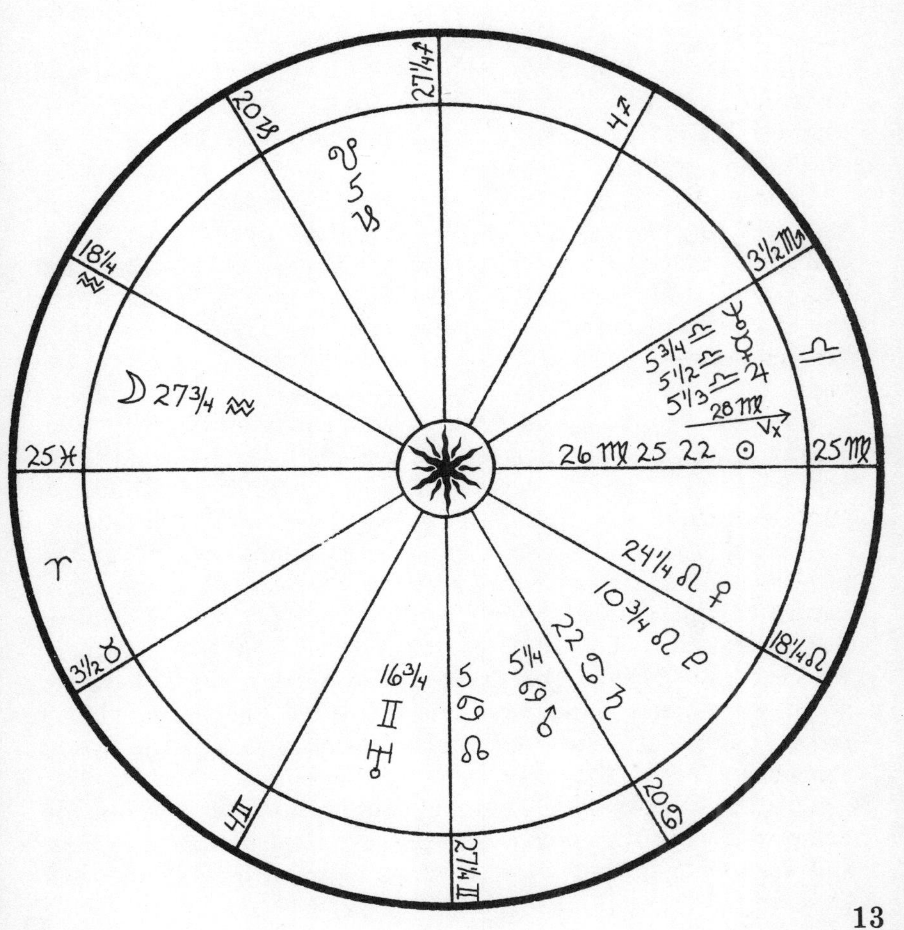

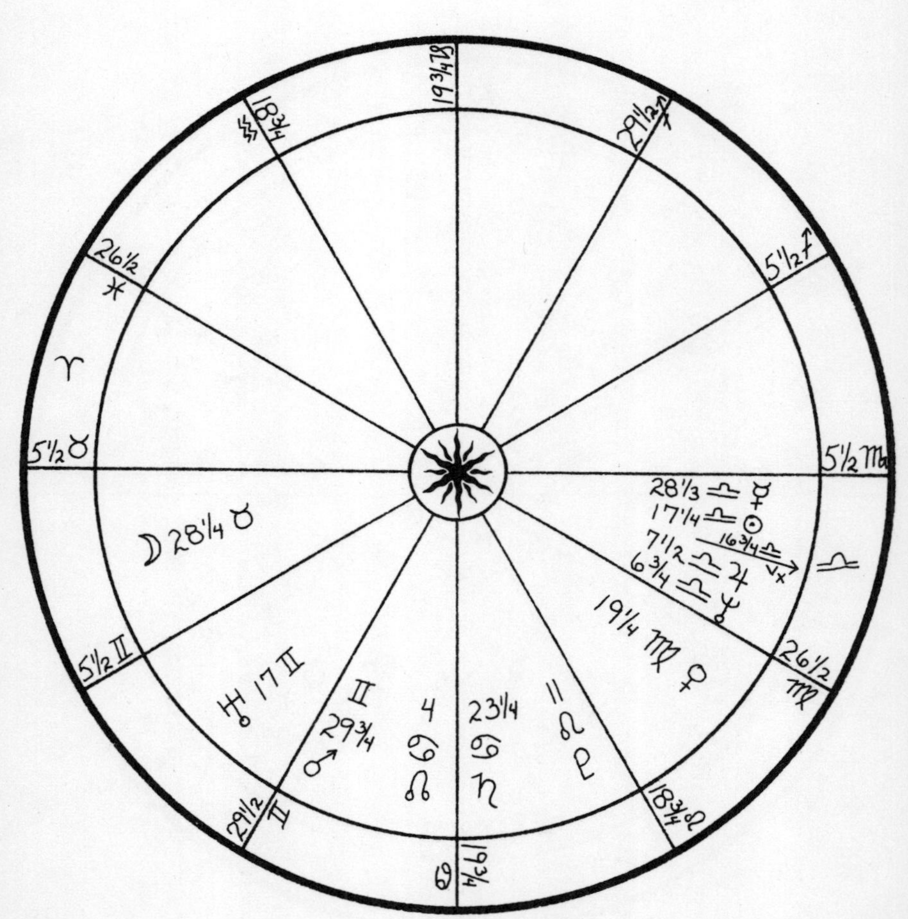

Figure 7
Couple
Progressed Composite
March 1966
New York City
Koch GOH Houses

Figure 8
Couple
Composite
Solar Return
1965
New York City
Koch GOH Houses

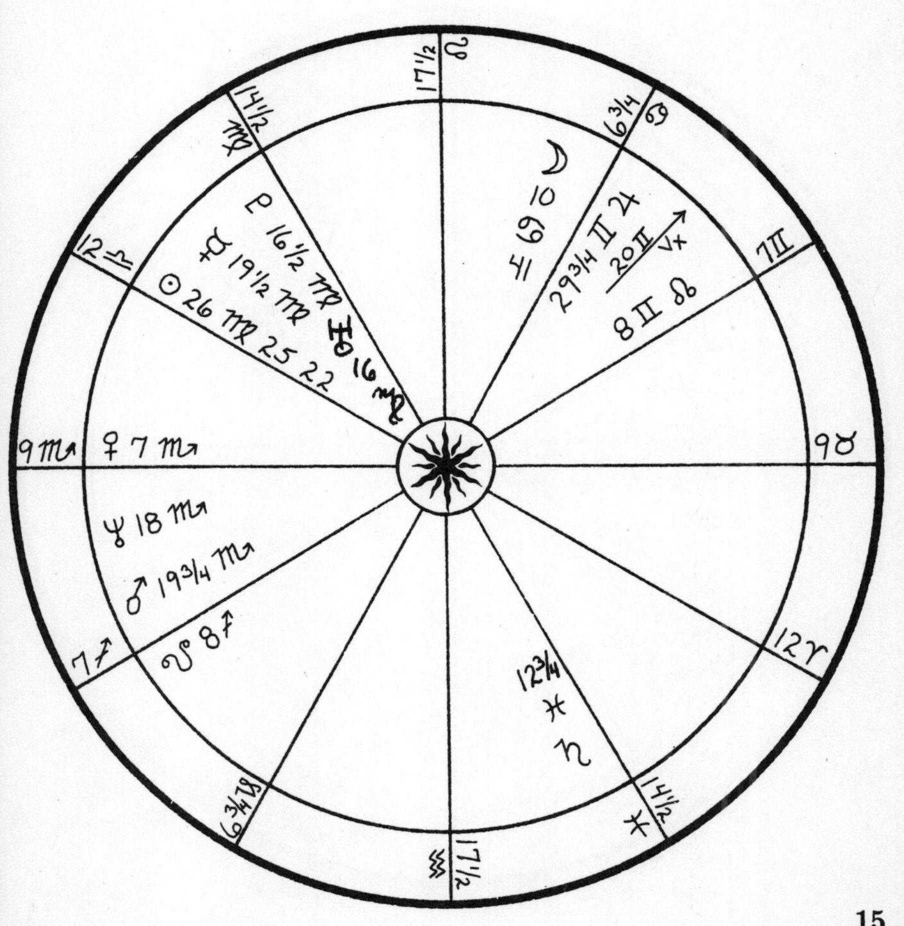

Figure 9
Composite
Mother and Daughter
New York City
Koch GOH Houses

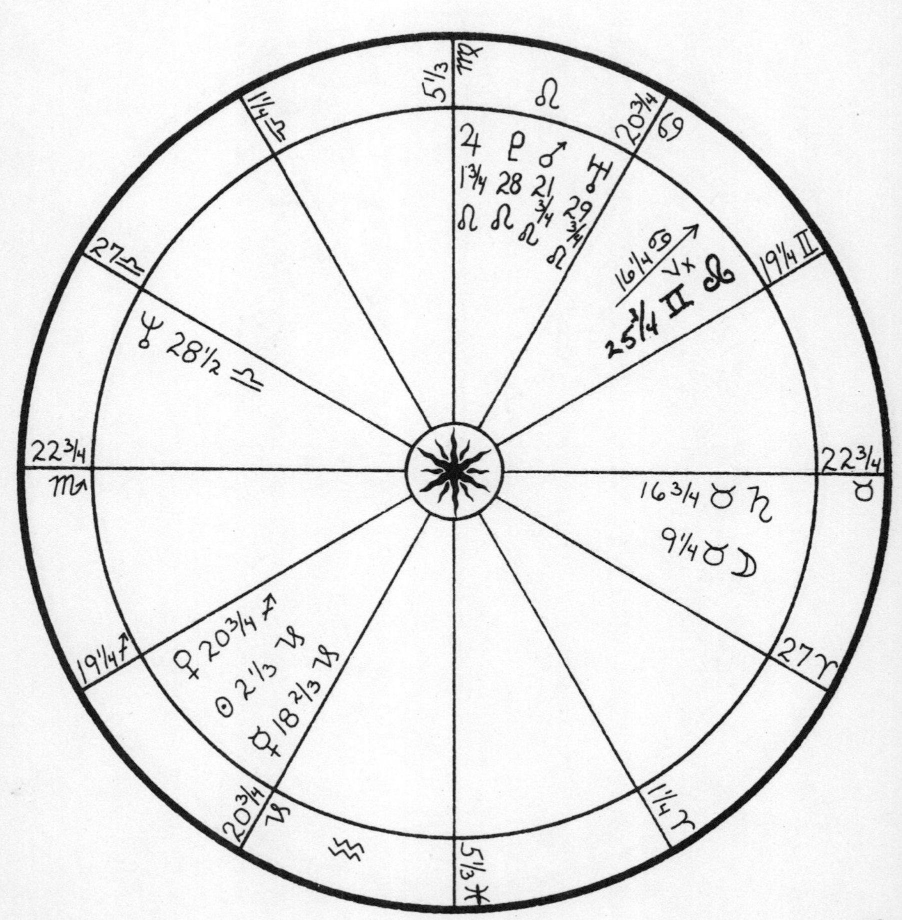

Figure 10
Composite
Father and Daughter
New York City
Koch GOH Houses

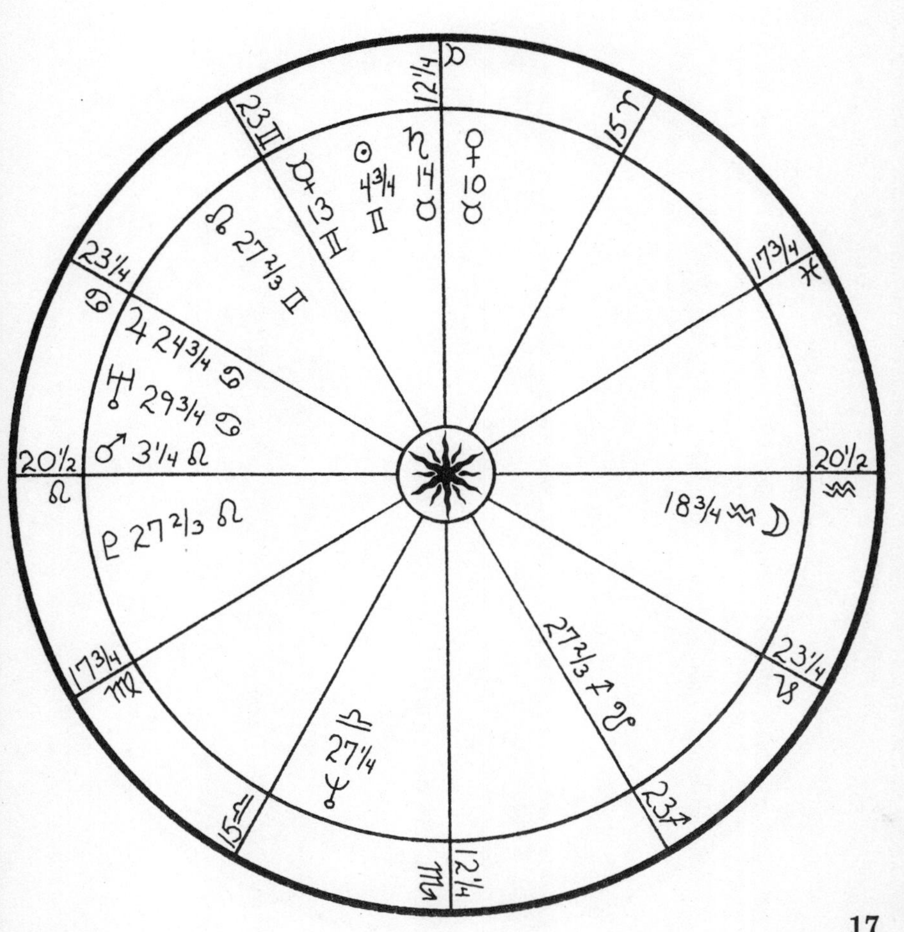

Mundane and
Semi-Mundane Composites

Mundane and Semi-Mundane Composites

Another rich area of composite work may be found in political and historical charts. An excellent example is the composite chart of the U.S.A. and the U.S.S.R. (Fig. 13). Used to make this composite is the Gemini rising U.S. chart in most common usage today (Fig. 11) and the time of the capture of the Leningrad telephone exchange and announcement of the new Soviet government (Fig. 12, fr. Donald Hey). Latitude used is 50°N. midway between Leningrad (60N) and Philadelphia (40N).

The ruler of the asc. square the asc—arguments, quarrelling. Jupiter in Gemini in the 3rd square its ruler Mercury—endless windy propaganda (on both sides) and half-truths. Saturn conjunct the Sun—over-serious, deadly earnest, humourless relations. Saturn (with the Sun) quincunx Uranus (with Pluto), 6-12—endless, driven scientific (Saturn, Uranus) competition focusing on weapons (sixth house, armies, etc.) of universal destruction and undoing (twelfth house), specifically atomic (uranium and plutonium!). Nodes on the asc.-desc.—a relationship of great responsibility, universal karma, if you will. Moon in Scorpio in the 7th—an active relationship, but guarded and most actions of importance worked out in secret. And so on by rulerships, etc . . .*

Some transits of note: The cold war commenced as Neptune conjoined the vertex and continued as it passed through the 7th (spies, spies, spies), only ending when it finally reached the 8th. When Pluto crossed the composite Venus, radical rearrangements of trade and monetary policies occurred, the beginnings of detente. Currently, Pluto is transiting the vertex (Nixon's nodes are here, as well), so certainly some major rearrangement is in the works.

Progressed composites and composite solar returns for various years of crisis are also of considerable interest and merit the attention of mundane astrology enthusiasts. A great deal can be gleaned about past and future foreign policy by the use of these techniques.

Another valuable application of composite charts is the construction of composites between a ruler or politician and the domain which he governs. The example here is a composite of John V. Lindsay, former mayor of New York City, and New York City. (Fig. 16). The New York City chart is cast for the time of the unification of the five boroughs into metropolitan New York (Fig. 14). Lindsay's chart is from data supplied by an aide while he was still a New York Congressman.

Moon conjunct Neptune would suggest some idealization and confusion, particularly in areas of communication (3-9). The opposition to Uranus would cause this to erratically switch on and off, or reverse direction. Saturn on the asc. might indicate government in general and perhaps long-term difficulties.

The transits seem to tell the story on this one. He first gained office as Jupiter transited the composite Vertex and shortly thereafter the Moon-Neptune conjunction. This is also the city's midheaven, so everyone was happy and much talk was about of great new changes to come.

The 1969 election was a different story. In the late spring primary, Lindsay was rejected as a candidate by his own party (trans. Saturn opposing the comp. asc. on the comp. 7th cusp). By the fall, however, the composite chart had a Jupiter return (and shortly after Jupiter over the asc.) and Lindsay won on an independent ticket.

By 1972, the love affair between Lindsay and the city began to come to an end. Neptune transited his ascendant, making him subject to all kinds of deceit and corruption from those around him and making his own public position unclear to the press. Meanwhile, transiting Saturn moved to oppose the composite Venus, Mercury, and Sun, then to conjoin the composite vertex and Pluto, bringing the mayor's popularity to an all-time low. Any good astrologer, by the use of this technique, could have estimated with fair certainty that Lindsay would face severe setbacks during his second term.

Again, as in all other instances, progressed composites and composite solar returns fill in many valuable details. All in all, mundane and semi-mundane composites can prove a very useful tool to the astrologer trying to navigate the swamps of modern politics.

*It might be noted, in passing, that the U.S.S.R.'s solar return very frequently coincides with the U.S.'s Election Day in November.

Figure 11
U.S.A.
Koch Birthplace Houses

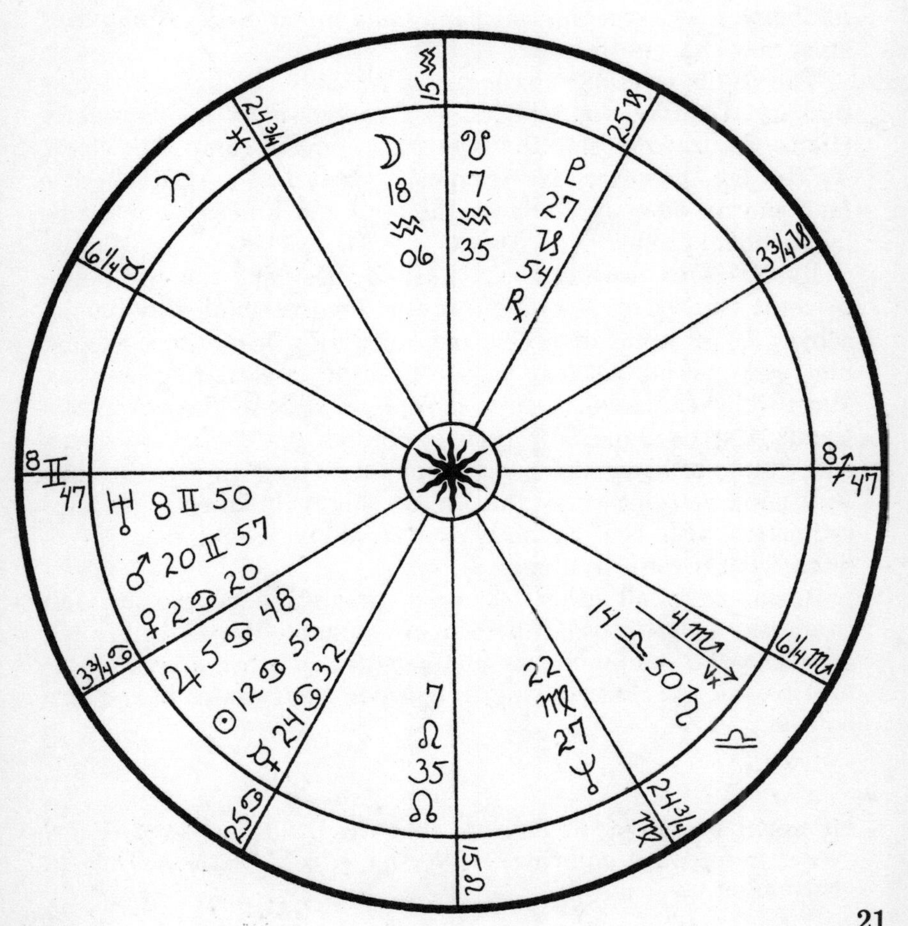

15 ♒
24¾ ♓
♈
6¼ ♉
☽ 18 ♒ 06
♋ 7 ♒ 35
♇ 27 ♑ 54 ℞
25 ♑
3¾ ♑
8 ♊ 47
♅ 8 ♊ 50
♂ 20 ♊ 57
♀ 2 ♋ 20
♃ 5 ♋ 48
☉ 12 ♋ 53
☿ 24 ♋ 32
3¾ ♋
25 ♋
7 ♌ 35 ☊
15 ♌
8 ♐ 47
14 ♎ 50 ♄
4 ♏ ☊
6¼ ♏
22 ♍ 27 ♆
♐
24¾ ♍

Figure 12
U.S.S.R.
Koch Birthplace Houses

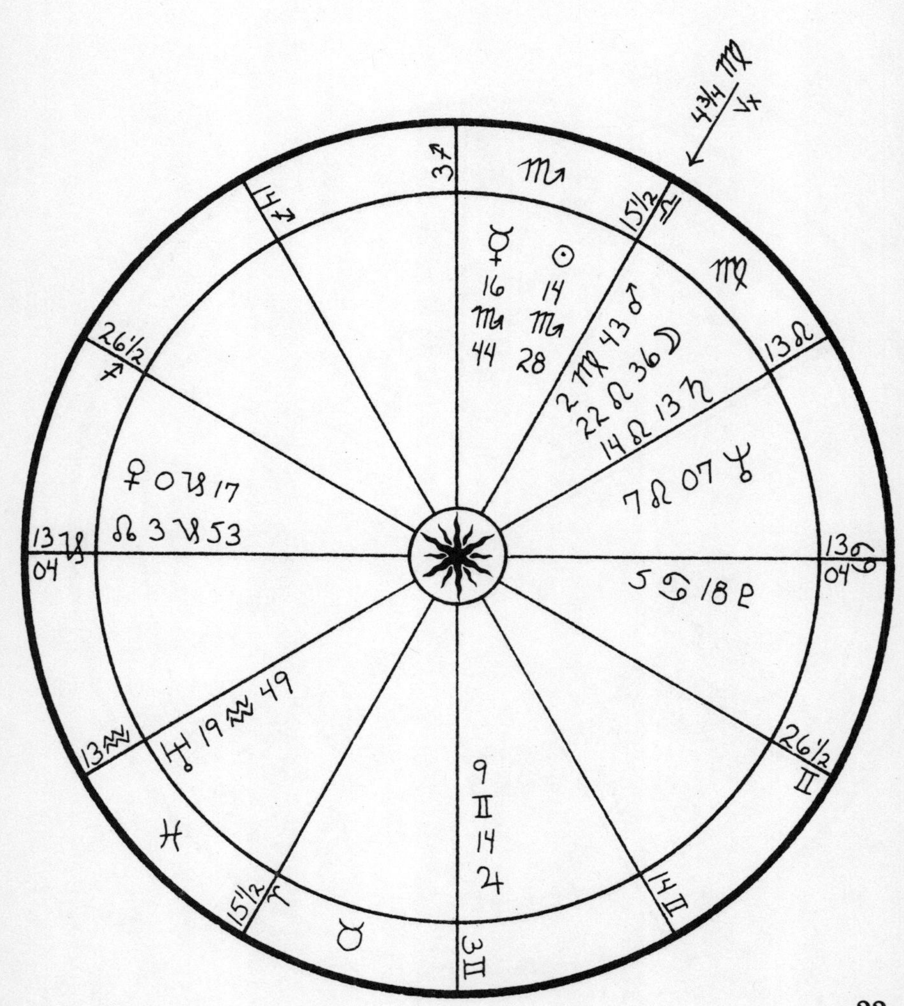
4¾ ♍
Vx
3 ♐
♐ 14
♏
26½
♐
♃ 0 ♑ 17
☊ 3 ♑ 53
13 ♑
04
13 ♒
♅ 19 ♒ 49
♓
15½
♈
♉
15½
♉
9
♊
14
♃
3 ♊
14 ♊
26½
♊
13 ♋
04
5 ♋ 18 ♇
7 ♌ 07 ♆
13 ♌
2 ♍ 43 ♂
22 ♌ 36 ☽
14 ♌ 13 ♄
♍
15½
☌
♉ ☉
16 14
♏ ♏
44 28
♏

Figure 13
U.S. and U.S.S.R.
Composite
Koch Birthplace Houses

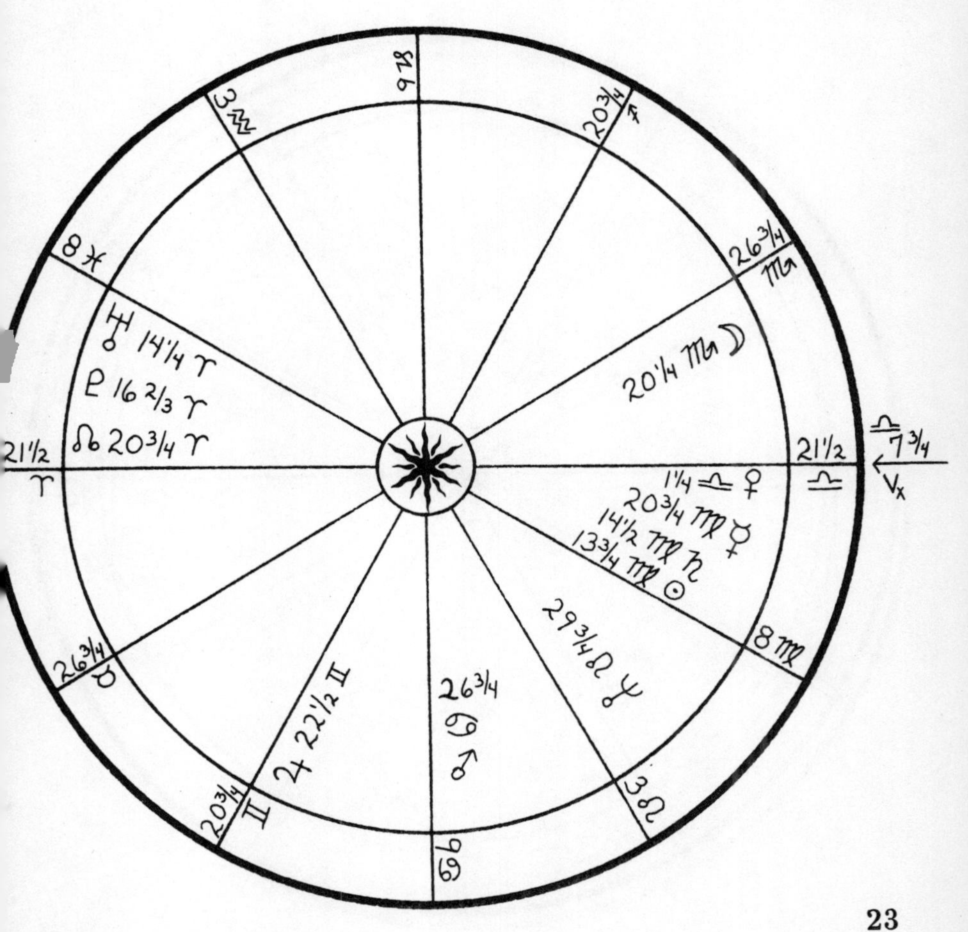

Figure 14
New York City
1 January 1898
O:00:00 Hours
Koch GOH Houses

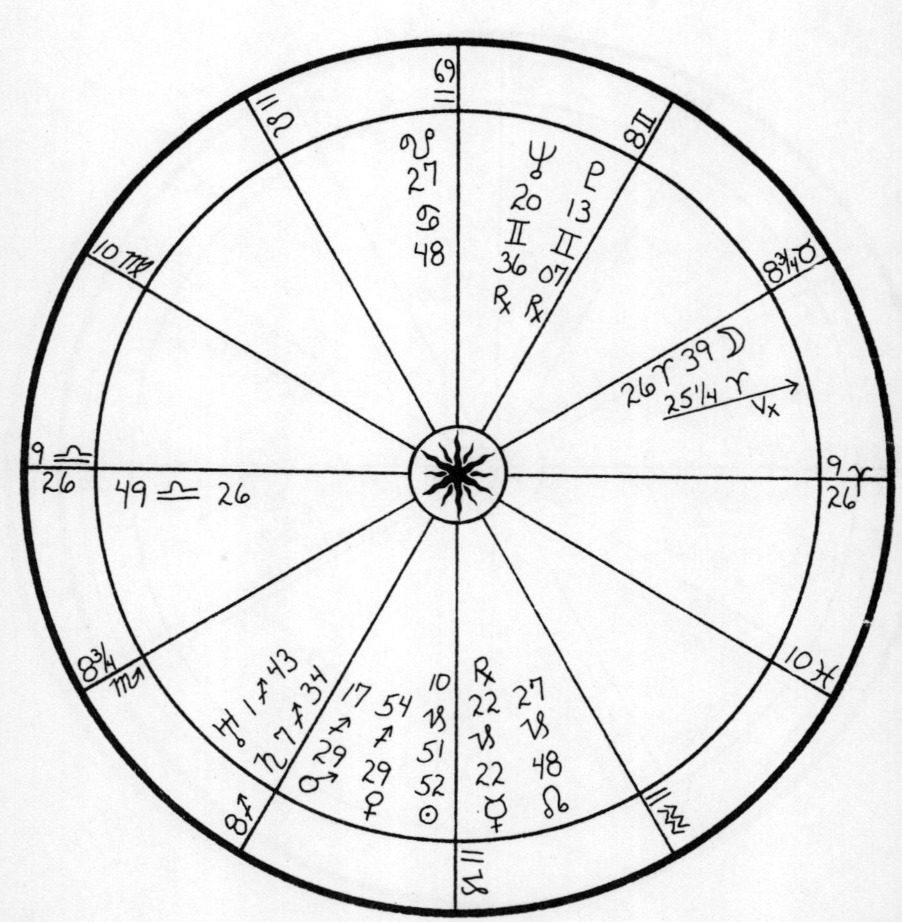

Figure 15
John Lindsay
24 November 1921, 7A.M.
New York City
Koch GOH Houses

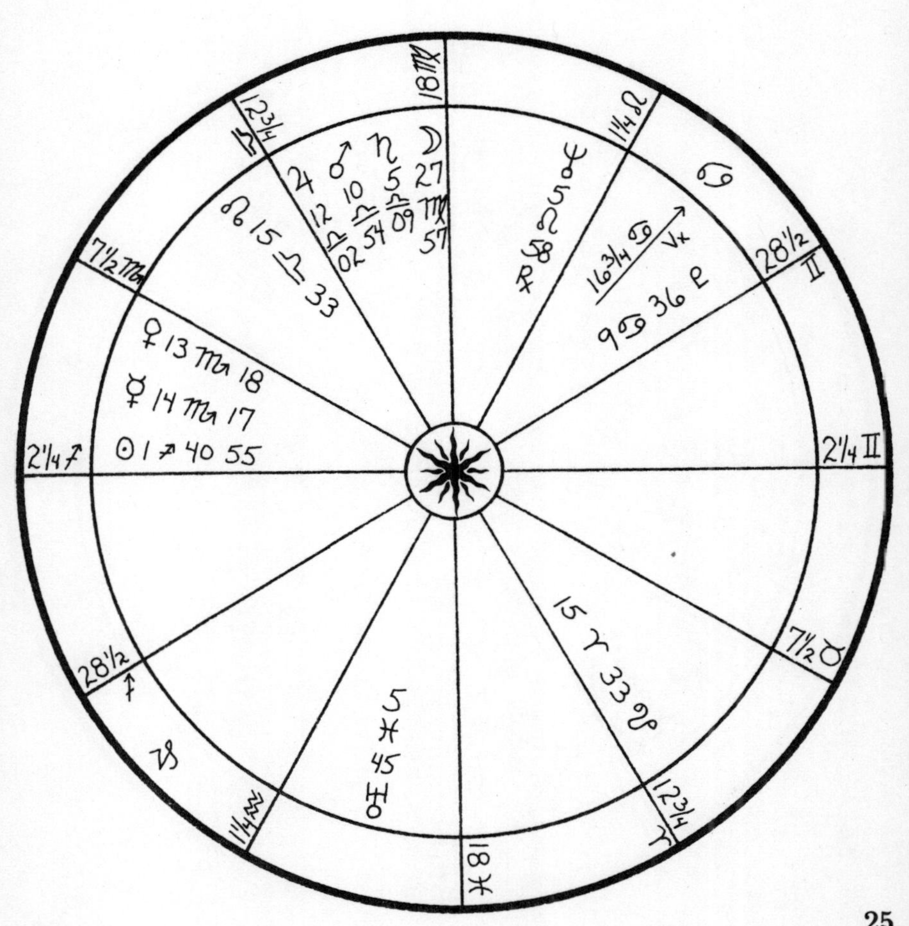

Figure 16
Composite
New York City and John Lindsay
New York City
Koch GOH Houses

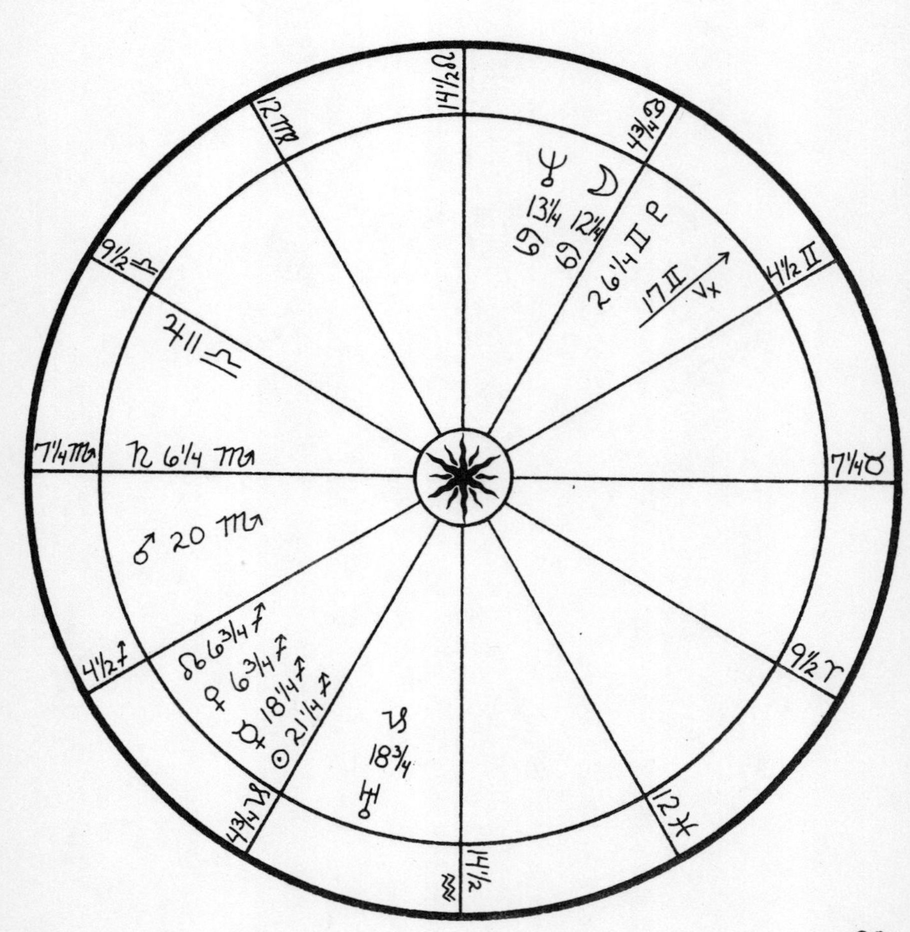

26

Multiple Composites

Multiple Composites

If more than two nativities are being used to construct a composite, merely add up the degrees past 0° Aries of each MC, Light or planet in question and divide by the number of nativities involved, thus creating a mean or average point. In this case, since there can be no near or far midpoints, all the positions of houses, signs, and bodies become completely bipolar and should be read as such (e.g., the first and seventh houses become interchangeable, opposing signs blend, etc.).

An excellent example of a multiple composite chart is that of the Beatles. Here is a heavy stellium in 2-8 houses—definitely the wealthiest musical group in history. Pluto is posited in 1-7 houses, mass media and mass reaction. Pluto-Venus rule the MC which meets the conjunction (4-10) of Saturn and Uranus—the Beatles were the most original and succinct musical creation of their time, as well as having the most appeal. In addition, the Moon (the people) and Saturn (endurance) rule the chart. One could hardly ask for more.

When the Beatles' composite is progressed to the time of their initial success in 1963, the vertex conjoins the North Node (two points of fate in conjunction), the Moon conjoins Pluto (both significators of the people), and Neptune rules the chart (one may recall that the early Beatles were very mysterious and secretive about themselves). In addition, the progressed 1-7 house cusps conjoin the natal composite vertex, the Sun is in 2-8 disposing of Pluto and the Moon, and Mars and Mercury conjoined and disposed by Venus are angular 1-7.

When the Beatles' composite is progressed to the time of their breakup in the summer of 1970, the vertex has moved to conjoin Neptune in 1-7, and the North Node conjoins the 1-7 cusps, marking fateful confusion and disarray in partnership. This period is also marked by several progressions within the individual Beatles' charts that indicate a move toward independence. Of great note here, however, is the sudden shift of the progressed composite Sun into the fifth house when George Harrison's progressed Sun moved from Pisces into Aries in 1967-68. It was at this time that he temporarily left the Beatles to study with Ravi Shankar in India. During this period each of the Beatles began to explore new independent careers that eventually led to the demise of the group as a whole.

Also of note is the two-way composite of Lennon and McCartney, the prominent songwriters and leaders of the group. Here is the Mars-Mercury conjunction that marked the articulate creative center of the group. They were, however, a songwriting team in name only, writing most of their material separately, as indicated by Venus square the ascendant (such a composite would not suggest cooperative creativity but rather financial arrangement—Moon in 7th but Sun in 5th, Saturn-Uranus in 2nd, Mars-Mercury in 6th).

This is but a brief introduction to multiple composite charts. The possibilities that lie herein are endless, from corporations to whole communities. The whole is more than the sum of its parts, and composite charts are an ample indication of the truth of that adage.

Figure 17
Multiple Composite Chart
The Beatles
London
Koch Birthplace Houses

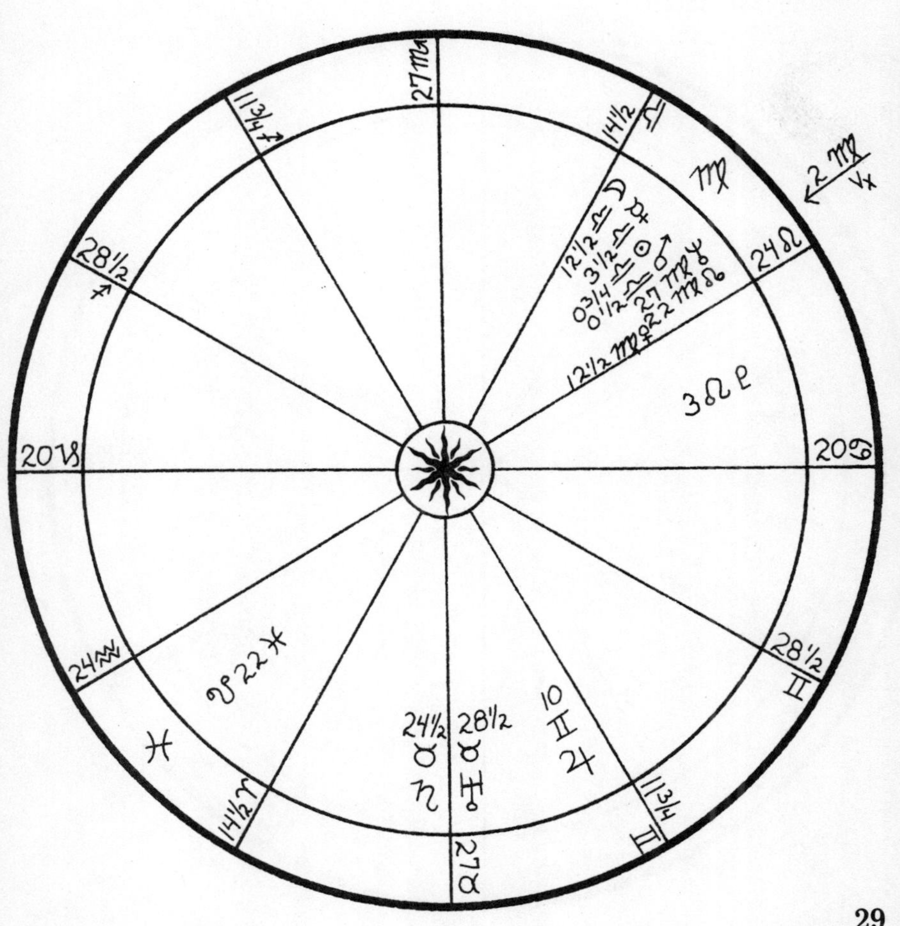

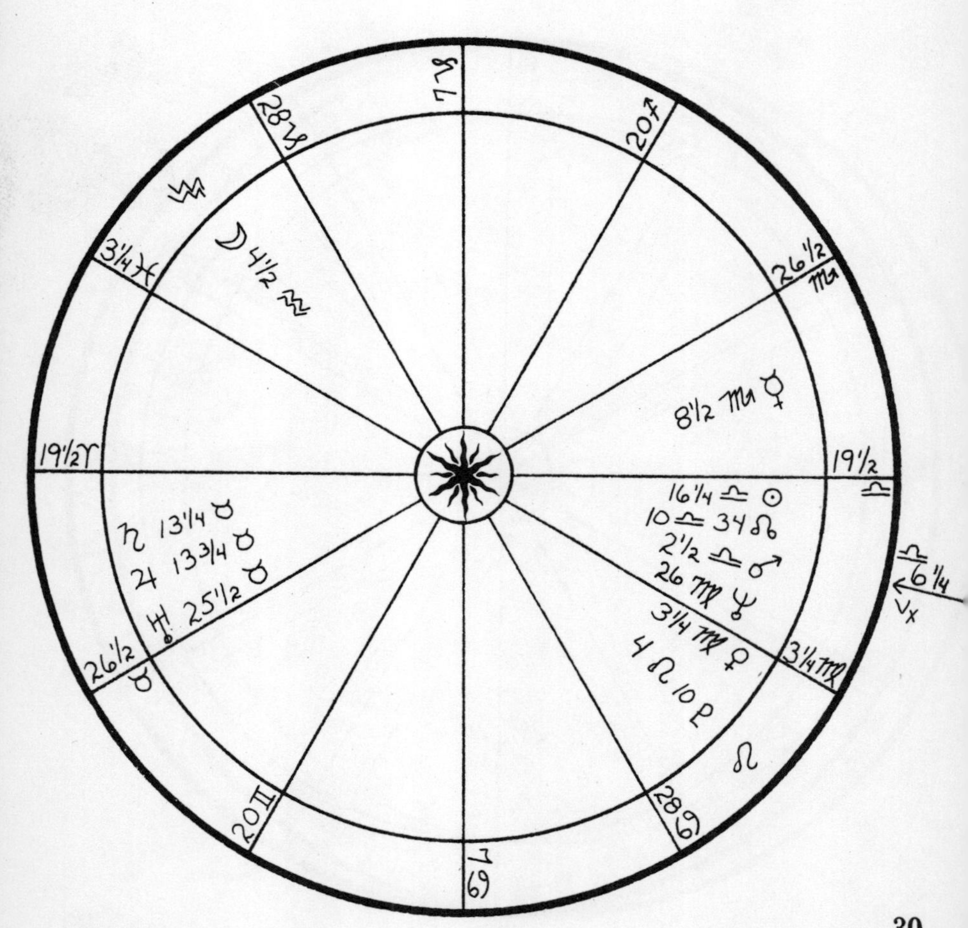

Figure 18A
John Lennon
9 October 1940
6:30 P.M. GWT
Liverpool, England
Koch Birthplace Houses

Figure 18B
Paul McCartney
18 June 1942
Midnight (rectified)
Liverpool, England
Koch Birthplace Houses

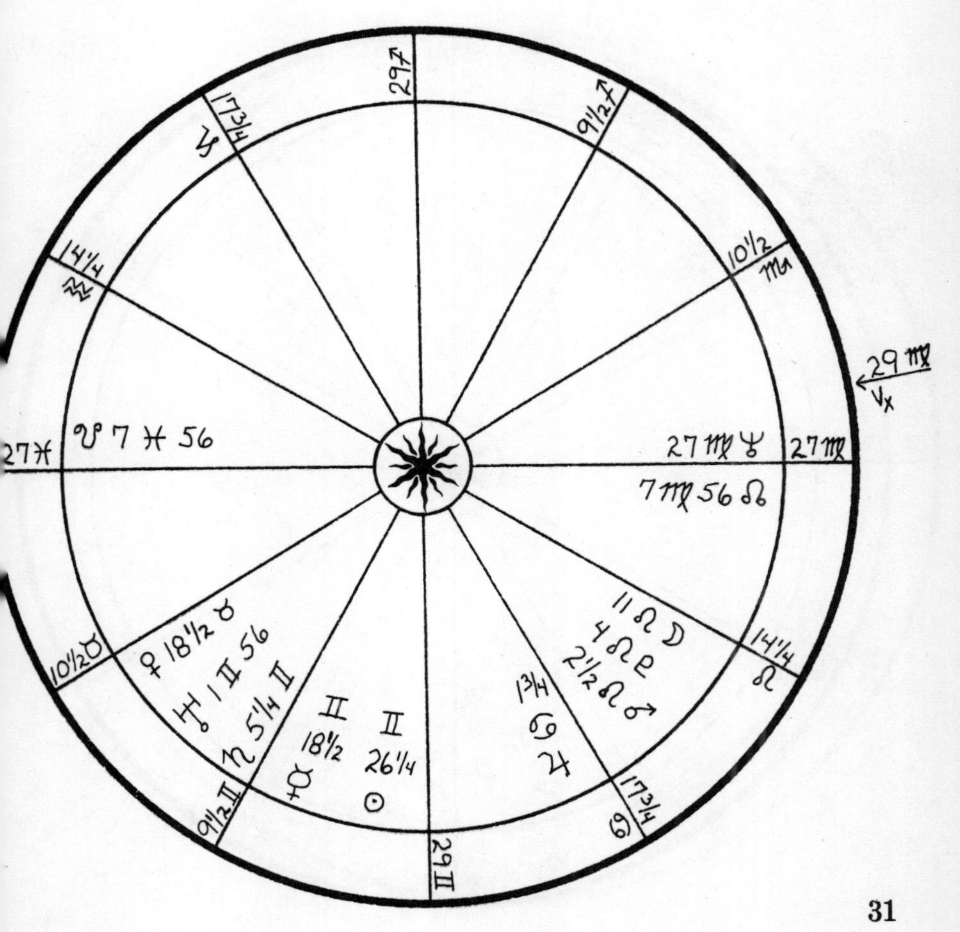

Figure 18C
George Harrison
25 February 1943
0:05 A.M. GWT
Liverpool, England
Koch Birthplace Houses

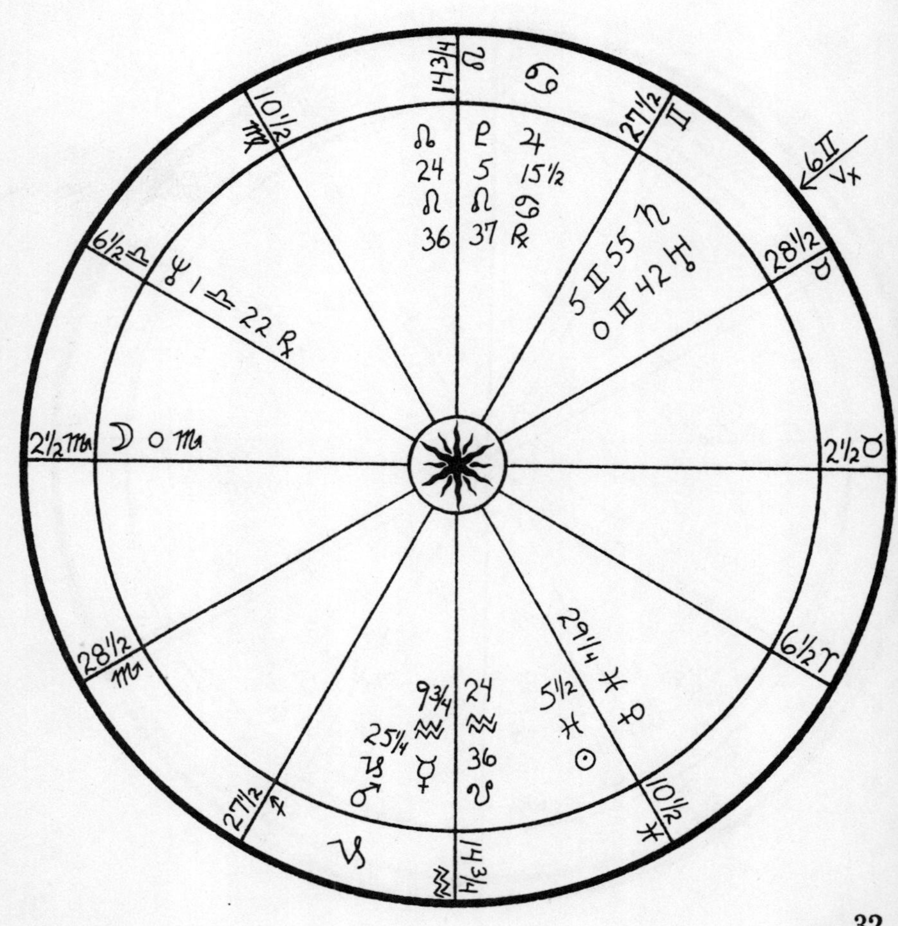

Figure 18D
Ringo Starr
7 July 1940
O:05 A.M. GWT
Liverpool, England
Koch Birthplace Houses

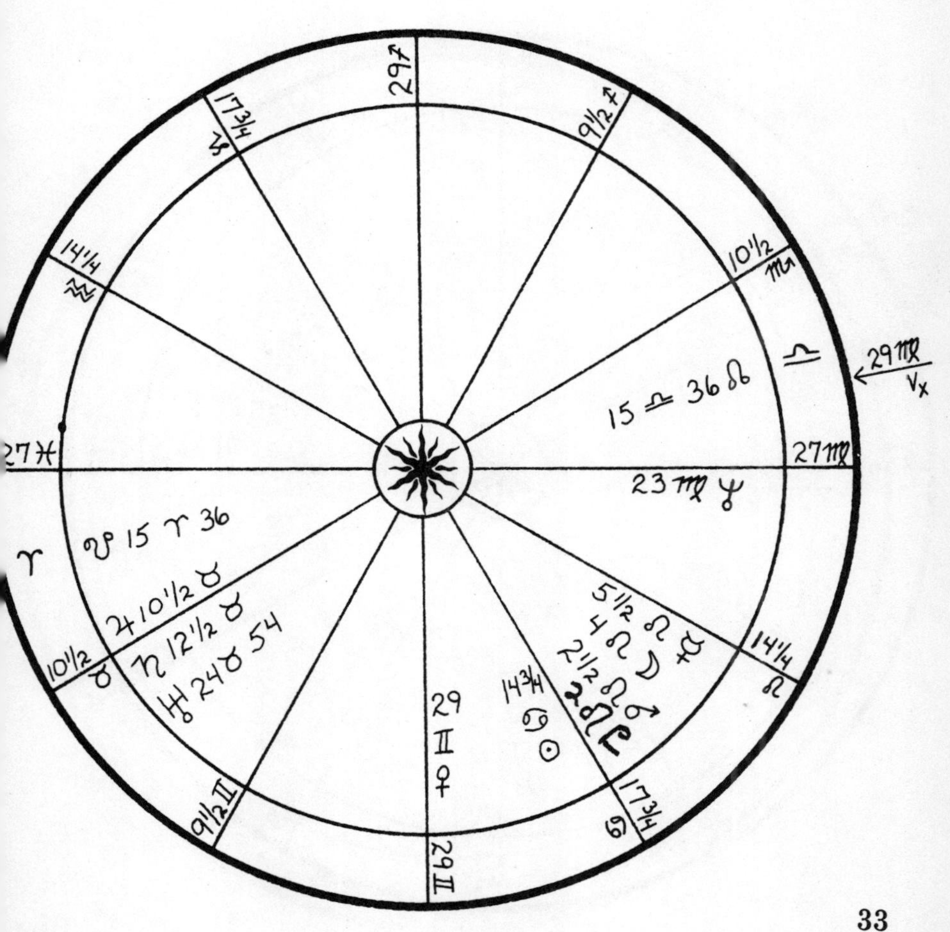

29♐
17¾ ♑
9½♐
14¼ ♒
10½ ♏
29 ♏ Vx
15 ♎ 36 ℞
27 ♓
27 ♍
23 ♍ ♆
♈ 15 ♈ 36
♃ 10½ ♉
5½ ♌
4 ♌
♄ 12½ ♉
2½ ♌
♅ 24 ♉ 54
14¼ ♌
10½ ♉
14¾ ♋
29 ♊
♀
♉ ☉
17¾ ♋
9½ ♊
29 ♊

Figure 19
Progressed Beatles Composite
Fall 1963
London
Koch Birthplace Houses

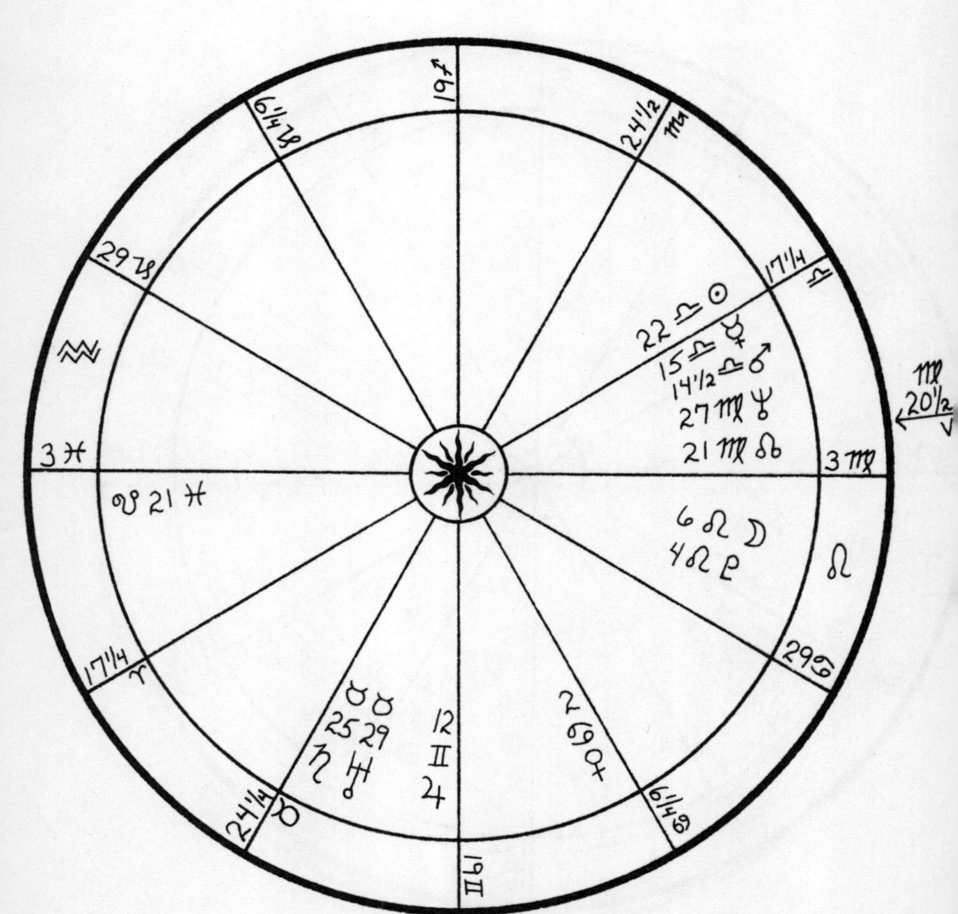

Figure 20
Progressed Beatles Composite
Summer 1970
London
Koch Birthplace Houses

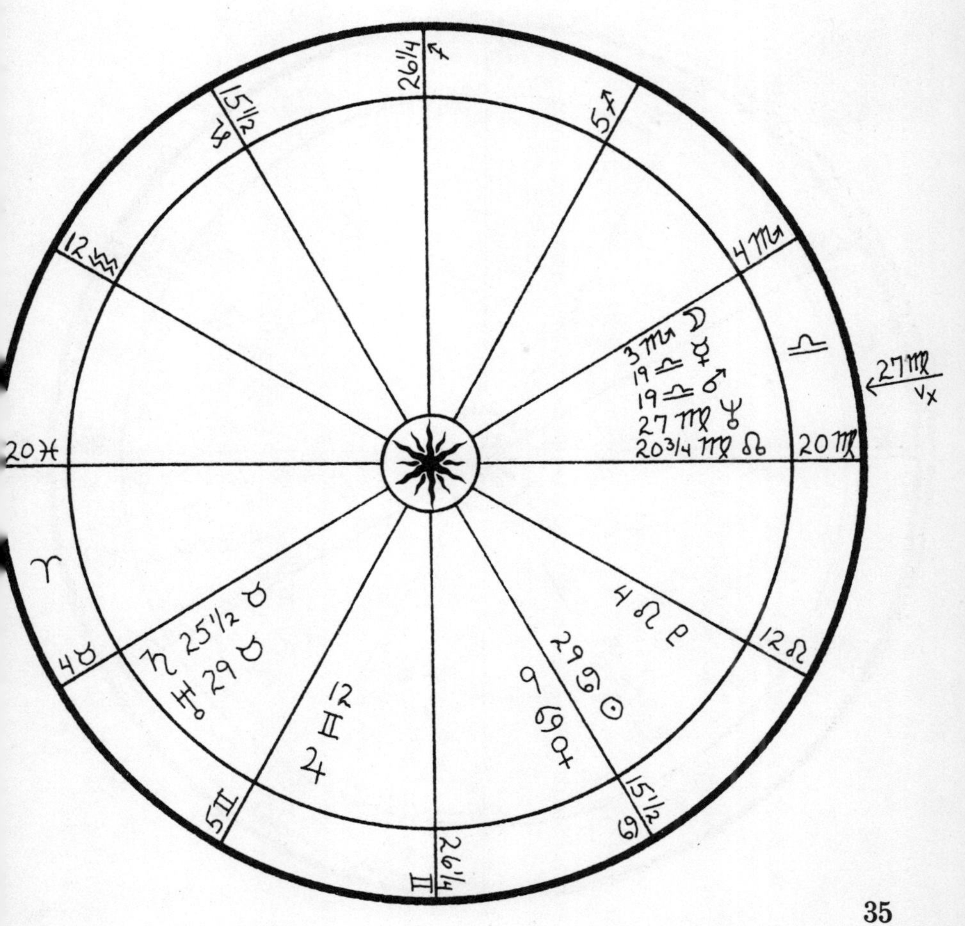

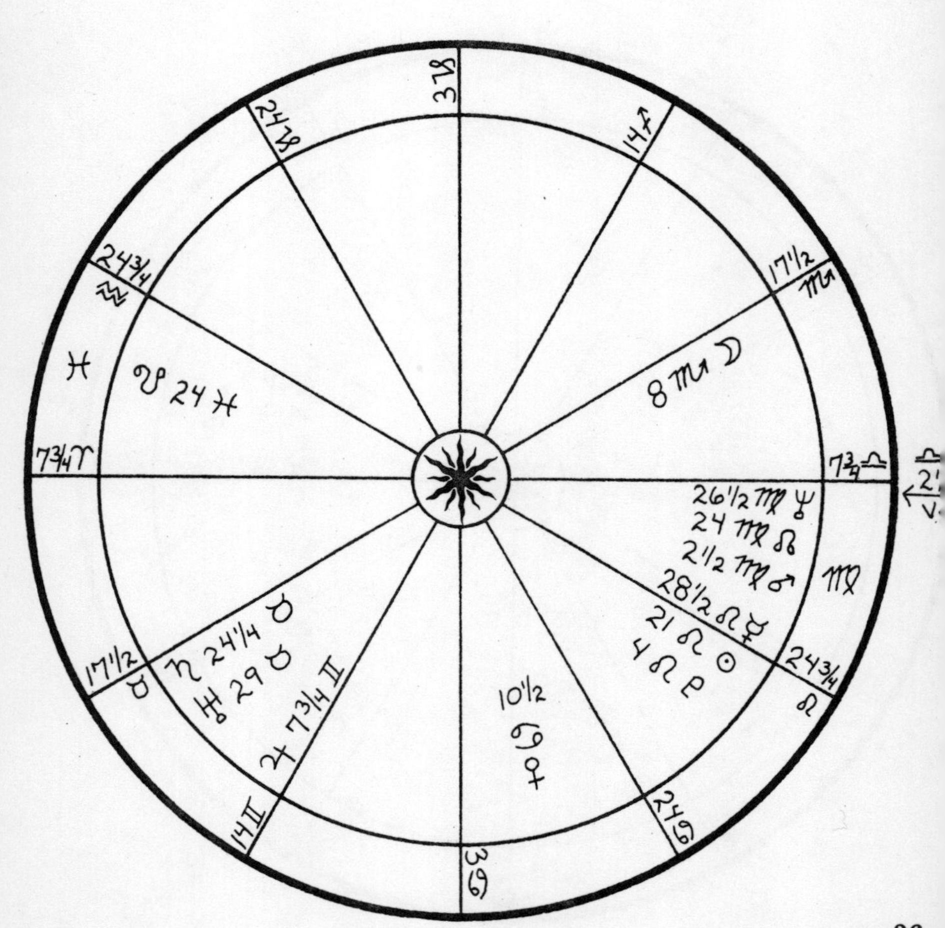

Composites for the Future

Composites for the Future

The possibilities for new varieties of composite charts seem endless, and sometimes it is difficult to know whether one is going off the deep end. For instance, in the composite charts of three champion Sealyham terriers (two males and one female) the couple with a Saturn-afflicted composite produced a small and unsatisfactory litter, while the same female bred with the other male where the composite features a grand trine of Jupiter and the Lights produced the largest Sealyham litter in history! Hmmmm . . .

Another fun game with composites is using your own chart to extrapolate the date of your ideal partner. For example: suppose you are a man (this works for a woman simply by reversing the Lights). Classical synastry would place your ideal partner's Sun on your Moon, and hopefully vice-versa. Since you know your Moon position, you know her Sun position (and her birthday) from which you can calculate the composite Sun. Providing you want an equal relationship, this composite Sun would also be the composite 7th house cusp (more frivolous souls might choose the 5th). From this it is easy to find the composite MC using the house tables at your own latitude. One more step tells you her MC (since the comp. MC is merely the midpoint between yours and hers) so you now can determine her exact time of birth. All that is needed is the birth year. Starting with your own birth year, page through your ephemeris checking the appropriate birthdays in the years surrounding (pick your own age range) and find one or two that have beneficial Moon, Venus, Mars (watch out for Saturn and Pluto!) contacts to your own chart. Now you will have at least one or two ideal sets of complete birth data—all it takes is a few newspaper ads and a *lot* of luck, and you've found your perfect partner! . . .

Another possibility is suggested by colleague Michael Jordan. It is called the Composite Point. It is derived by adding up the ten Lights and planets of a horoscope and dividing by ten. The result is an individual degree that seems to respond to transits and progressions in a way somewhat similar to the vertex. The traditional symbolism associated with the particular degree and what fixed stars lie there are also very informative in interpreting the Composite Point.

Other possibilities? Perhaps composites of Johndro charts would work. Perhaps composites of natal and horary or electional charts. Composites of employees' charts with the company they work for. Corporate merger composites. Cities with countries (New York City composited with the U.S.A. chart is quite interesting). Astrologers with clients (this really helps). Jockeys with horses. Captains with ships. The list is inexhaustible. Within the basic midpoint philosophy upon which composite charts are based, any two things that have a valid horoscope may be composited with valid results, though the ensuing interpretation would depend entirely on the nature of the things composited.

Here in these pages I have set down an outline of the bulk of my experience with composites, to date, in hopes that other astrologers may use it as a beginning and go on to further the sophistication of an obviously useful technique (already this is being incorporated into a personality-matching computer program). It is an astrological tool that has sat too long on the shelf for lack of publicity, and I hope that, in the U.S.A., it is an idea whose time has come.

More Composite Examples

Richard Nixon
9:30 p.m.
9 January 1913
Yorba Linda, California
From Al H. Morrison

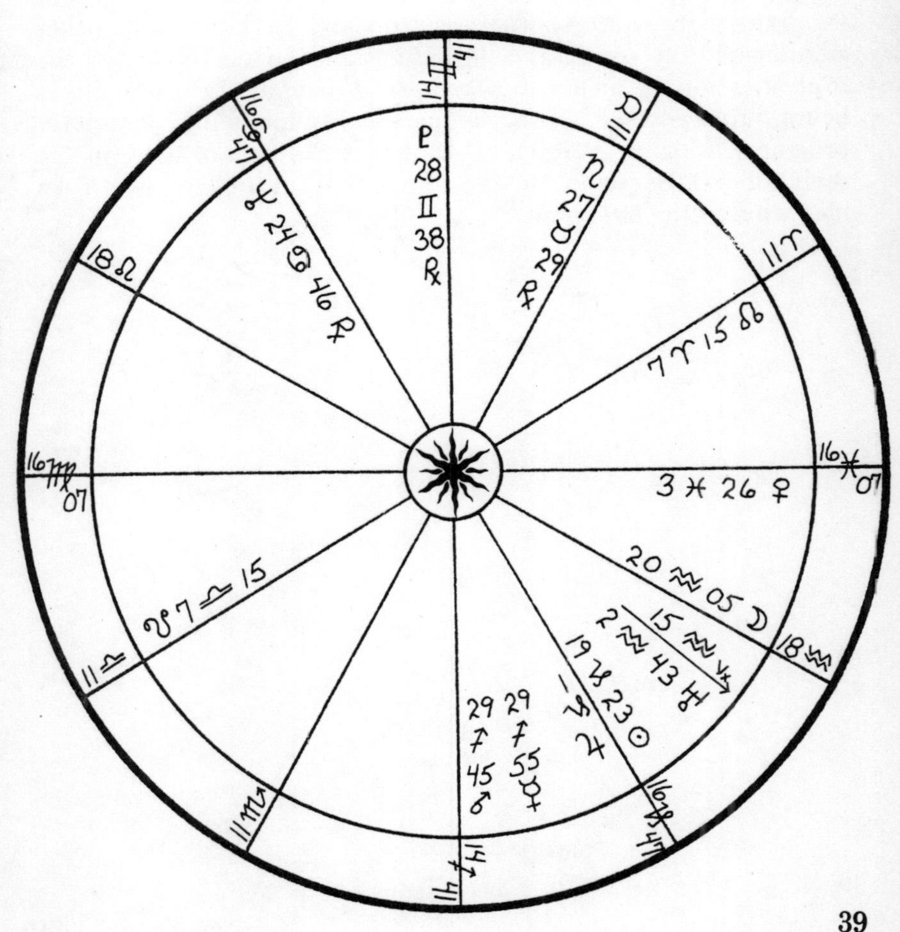

Officially declared beginning of
present Federal government
00:01 a.m.
4 March 1789
New York City
From Al H. Morrison

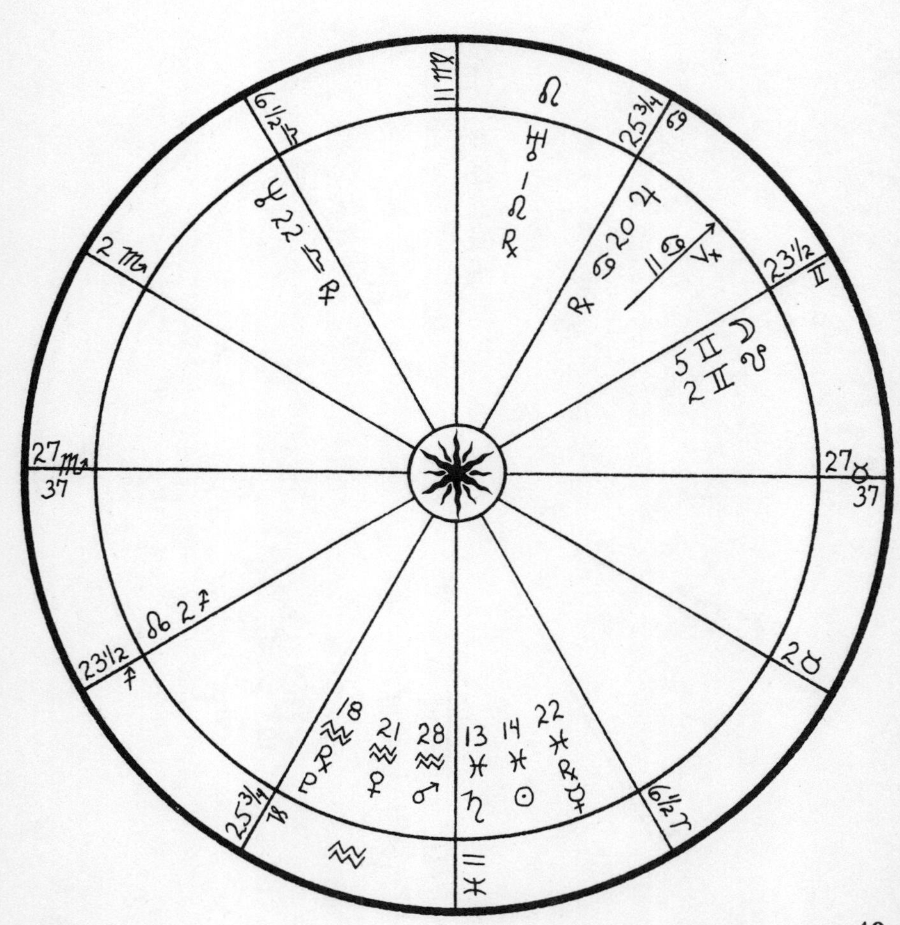

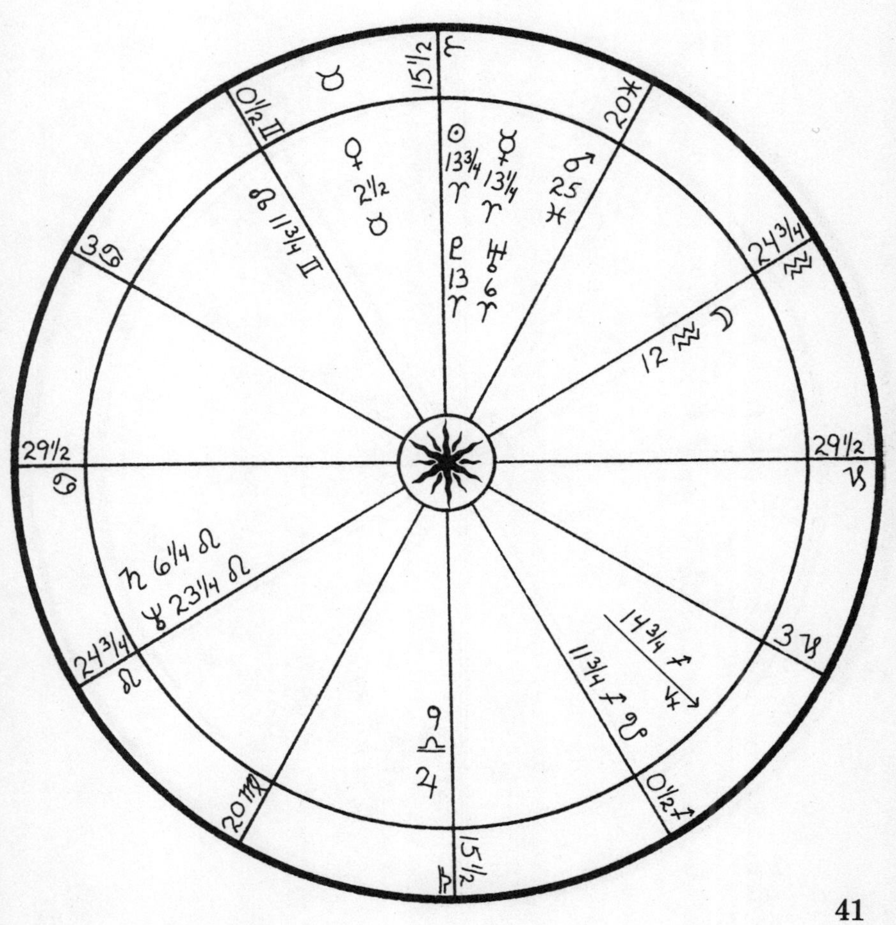

Composite
Nixon and Federal Government
Washington, D.C.

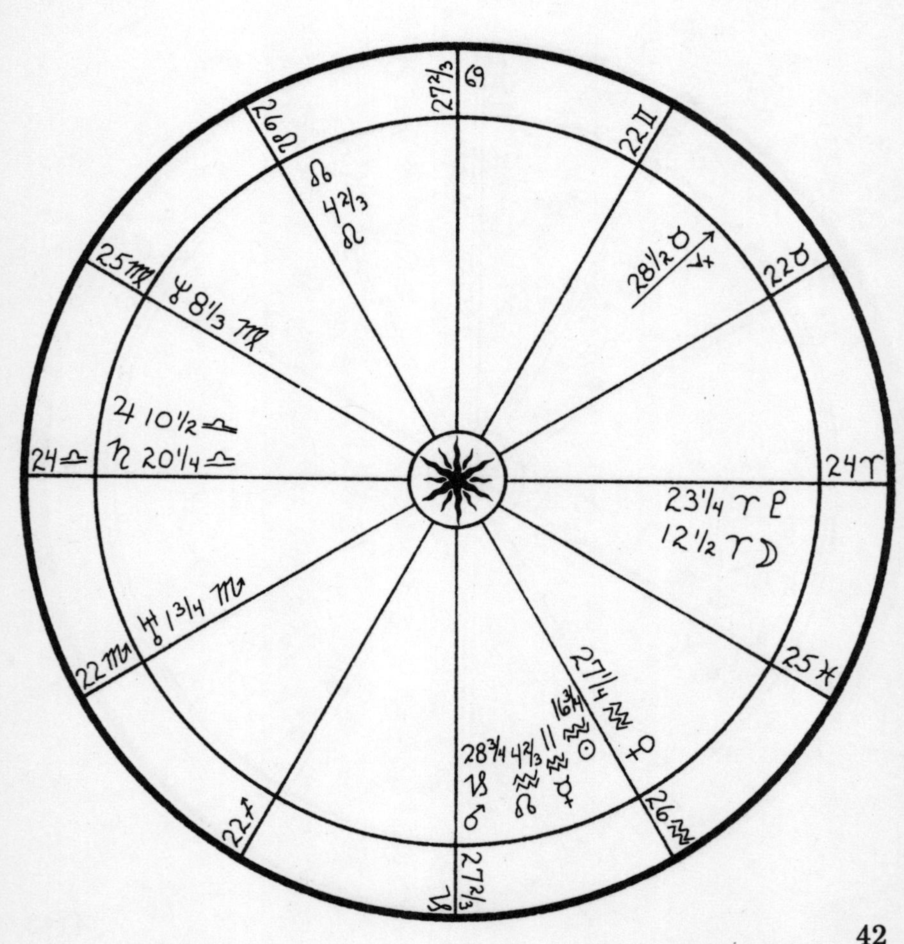

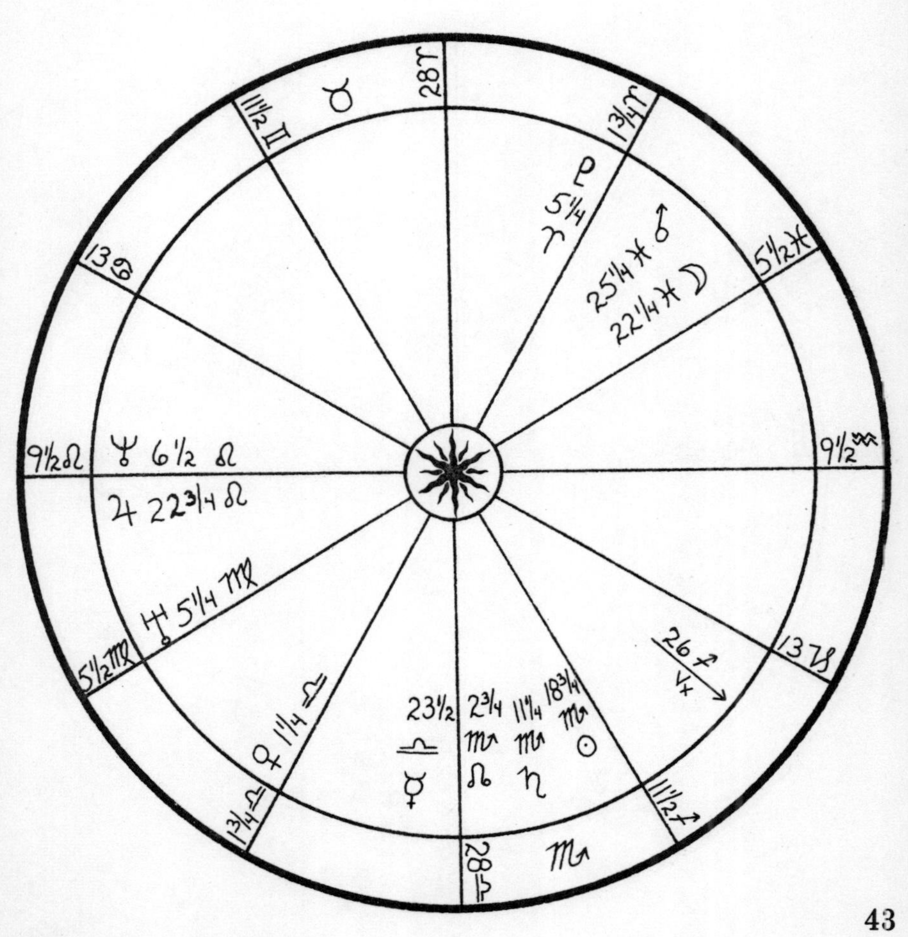

Adolf Hitler
20 April 1889
Braunau, Austria
From A.C. Emerson

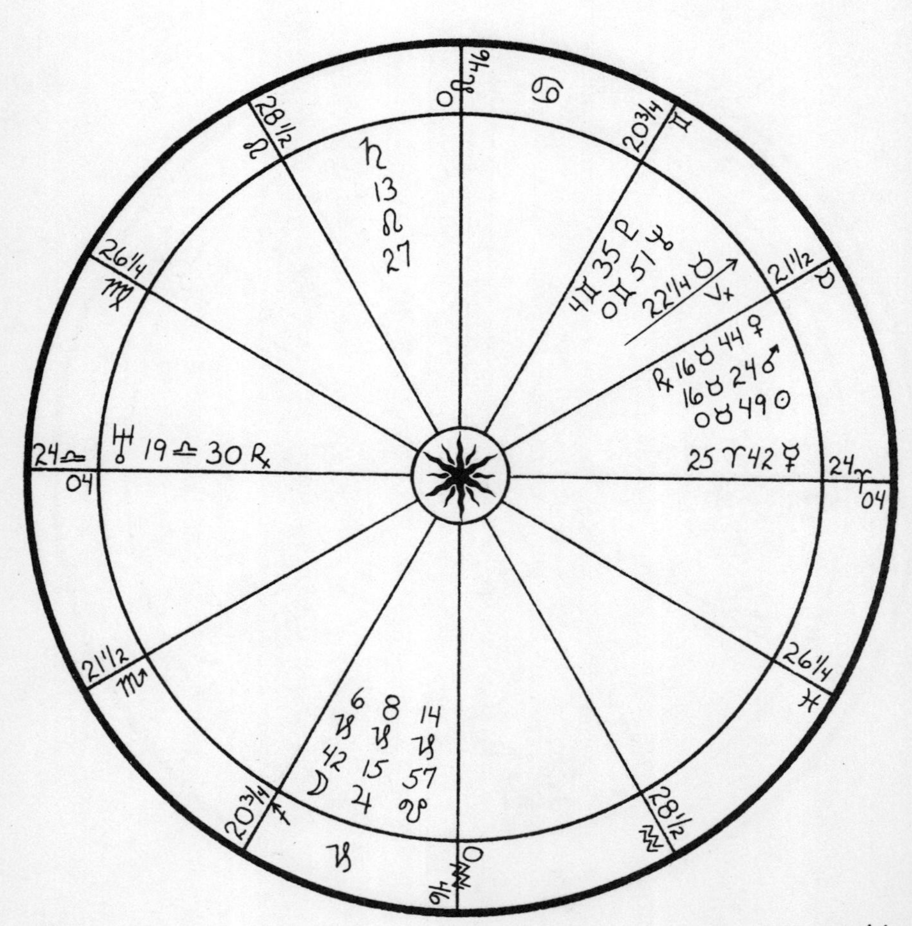

Eva Braun
5:31 a.m.
February 6, 1912
Munic
From M.E. Jones

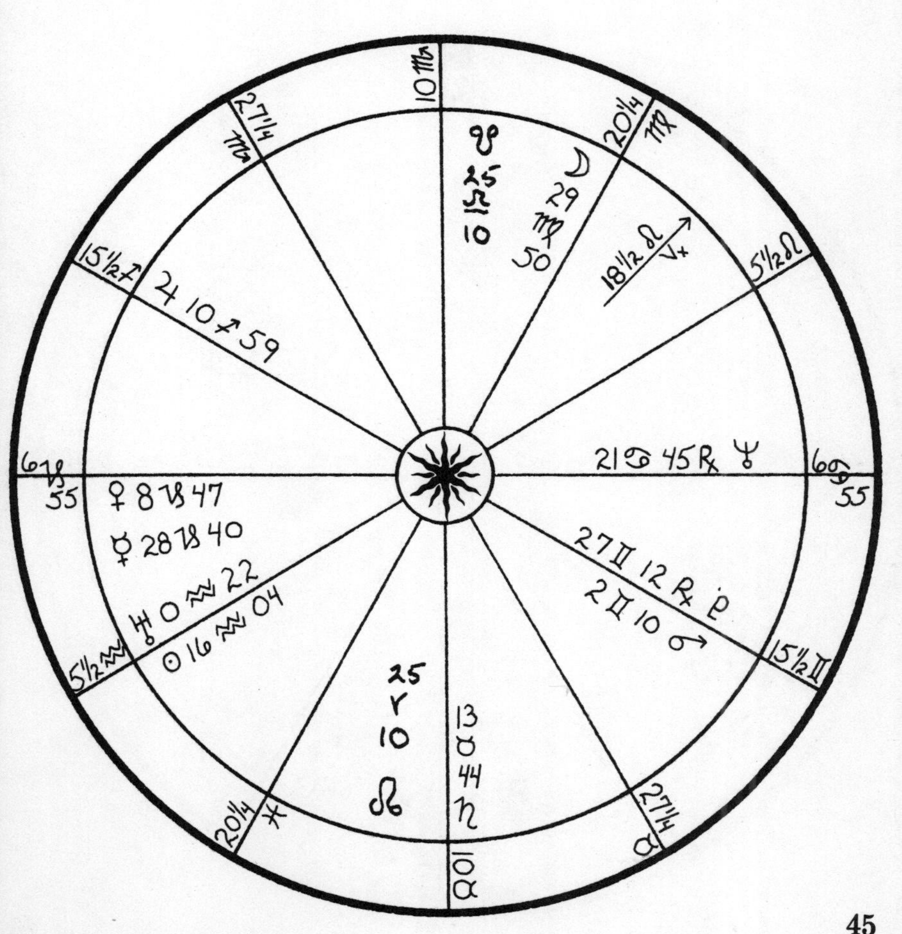

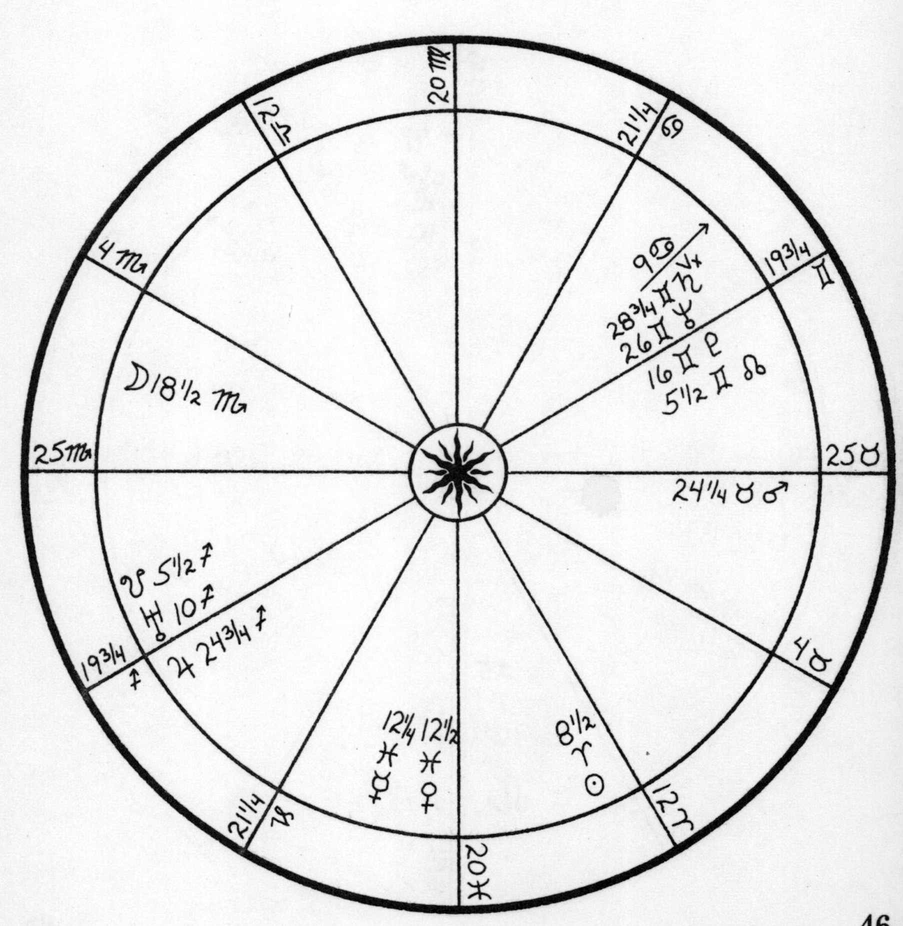

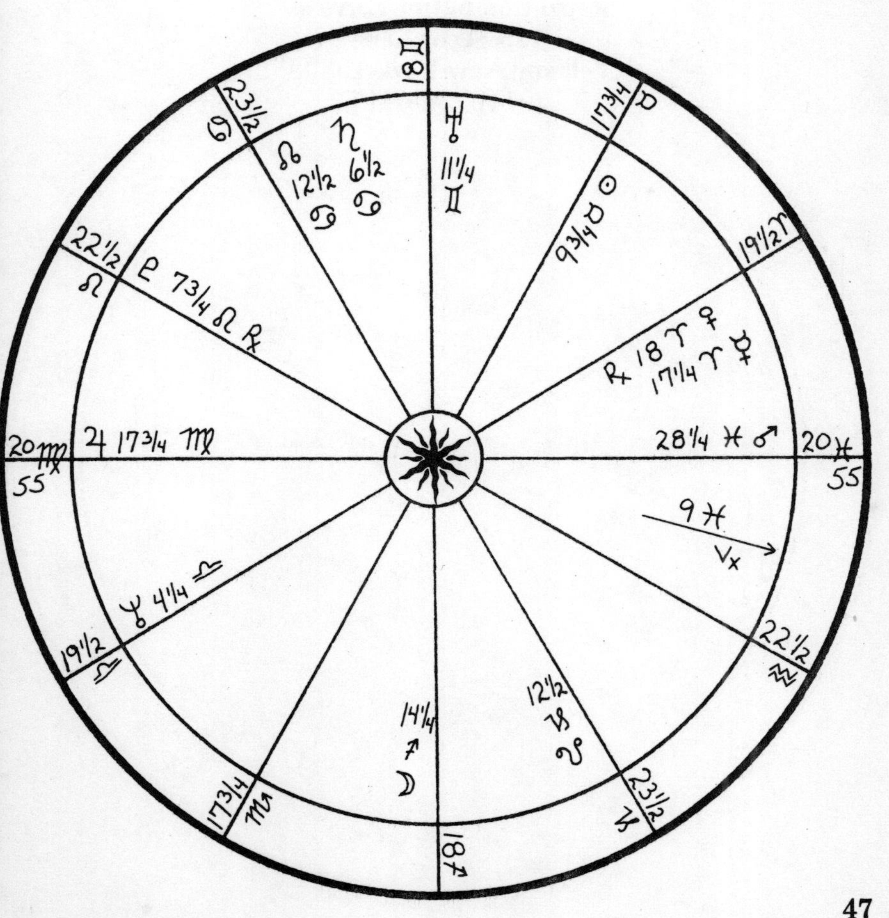

SPECIAL NOTE

For those too busy to do their own calculations, Neil Michelsen's Astro Computing Services also computes composite charts as well as other excellent services. For a two-way composite, just send in the birth data of the two nativities (exact time, of course, is essential) and you will receive the two natal charts complete with aspects and midpoints plus the composite. The special price for readers of this book is $5.00. A progressed composite $3.00, a composite solar return is $2.50. Multiple composite prices vary with the number of charts involved. Your choice of house system. This is the only computer service, to date, that does composites, so it's worth knowing about. Their address is:

Astro Computing Services
129 Secor Lane
Pelham, New York 10803
(914) 738-0717